Enchanted Forest Creatures

Invite a little magic into your life with lovable fantasy characters and woodland animals. These easy-to-crochet creatures are fun for all ages to collect and display in whimsical settings.

LEISURE ARTS, INC. • Maumelle, Arkansas

Fawn

EASY +

Finished Size: Approximately
9" tall x 9" long (excluding ears & tail) (23 cm x 23 cm)

SHOPPING LIST

Yarn (Medium Weight)

☐ Brown - 160 yards (146 meters)
☐ Tan - 18 yards (16.5 meters)
☐ Off White - 10 yards (9 meters)
☐ Black - small amount

Crochet Hook

☐ Size G (4 mm)

Additional Supplies

☐ Safety pin - optional
☐ Yarn needle
☐ Polyester fiberfill
☐ 12 mm Black safety eyes - 2
   (Please take caution if the
   toy is for a child that is at
   risk of choking. See Safety,
   page 45.)

GAUGE INFORMATION

Gauge is **not** of great importance as long as your crochet fabric is very dense *(see Gauge, page 44)*.

─── STITCH GUIDE ───

SINGLE CROCHET 2 TOGETHER
   (abbreviated sc2tog)

Pull up a loop in each of next 2 sc, YO and draw through all 3 loops on hook (**counts as one sc**).

Eye Patch (Make 2)

With Tan, ch 2, (2 sc, 2 dc, 2 sc, slip st) in second ch from hook; finish off leaving a long end for sewing.

Eyelid (Make 2)

With Tan, ch 3; finish off leaving a long end for sewing.

Head

Rnd 1 (Right side)**:** With Brown, make an adjustable loop to form a ring *(Figs. 1a-d, page 45)*; work 6 sc in ring; do **not** join, place marker to indicate beginning of rnd *(see Markers, page 45)*.

Rnd 2: 2 Sc in each sc around: 12 sc.

Rnd 3: (Sc in next sc, 2 sc in next sc) around: 18 sc.

Rnd 4: (Sc in next 2 sc, 2 sc in next sc) around: 24 sc.

Rnd 5: (Sc in next 3 sc, 2 sc in next sc) around: 30 sc.

Rnds 6-11: Sc in each sc around.

Rnd 12: (Sc2tog, sc in next 3 sc) around: 24 sc.

Rnd 13: (Sc2tog, sc in next 2 sc) around: 18 sc.

The loop can be slipped from the hook onto safety pin while attaching the eyes.

Insert the safety eyes through the beginning ch of the Eye Patch, then through Rnd 5 of the Head with the 2-dc pointed toward the last rnd worked and spacing the Eye Patches approximately 5 sc apart.

Use whipstitch *(Figs. 5a & b, page 46)* for the method of sewing to join the pieces together.

Sew Eyelids to Eye Patches above the safety eyes. Sew Eye Patches in place.

Stuff Head with polyester fiberfill.

Rnd 14: (Sc2tog, sc in next sc) around: 12 sc.

Rnd 15: Sc2tog around: 6 sc.

Continue to sc2tog around until hole is closed; slip st in next sc, finish off.

Neck

Work same as Head through Rnd 4: 24 sc.

Rnds 5-14: Sc in each sc around.

Slip st in next sc, finish off leaving a long end for sewing.

Muzzle

Rnd 1 (Right side)**:** With Brown, make an adjustable loop to form a ring; work 6 sc in ring; do **not** join, place marker.

Rnd 2: Sc in next 3 sc, 2 sc in each of next 3 sc: 9 sc.

Rnd 3: 2 Sc in each of next 3 sc, sc in next 6 sc: 12 sc.

Rnds 4-6: Sc in each sc around.

Slip st in next sc, finish off leaving a long end for sewing.

Nose

Row 1 (Right side)**:** With Black, ch 3, (dc, ch 3, slip st) in third ch from hook; finish off leaving a long end for sewing.

Mouth/Throat

Rnd 1 (Right side)**:** With Off White, ch 3, 11 dc in third ch from hook; join with slip st to top of beginning ch-3.

Rnd 2: Skip first dc, 3 dc in next dc, dc in next dc, 3 dc in next dc, skip next dc, slip st in next dc, skip next dc, 3 dc in next dc, dc in next dc, 3 dc in next dc, skip last dc; join with slip st to joining slip st, finish off leaving a long end for sewing.

Head Assembly

Stuff Muzzle and Neck with polyester fiberfill.

Use photos as guides for placement of all pieces. See Tips, page 45.

Sew Muzzle to Head under the Eye Patches.

Sew Nose to Muzzle.

Sew Neck to Head.

Sew Mouth/Throat across Muzzle, Head, and Neck placing the slip sts at the sides.

Ear (Make 2)

INNER EAR

With Off White, ch 7.

Row 1 (Right side)**:** Sc in second ch from hook, dc in next 4 chs, (sc, ch 2, sc) in last ch; working in free loops of beginning ch *(Fig. 3b, page 46)*, dc in next 4 chs, sc in next ch; finish off: 12 sts and 1 ch-2 sp.

Note: Loop a short piece of yarn around any stitch to mark Row 1 as **right** side.

OUTER EAR

With Brown, ch 9.

Row 1 (Right side)**:** Dc in third ch from hook, sc in next ch, dc in next 4 chs, (sc, ch 2, sc) in last ch; working in free loops of beginning ch, dc in next 4 chs, sc in next ch, dc in next ch: 14 sts and 1 ch-2 sp.

Joining Row: Ch 1, turn; sc in first dc, holding Inner Ear in front of Outer Ear, with **wrong** sides together, matching sts, and working through **both** loops on **both** pieces, sc in next 6 sts and in next ch, ch 2, sc in next ch and in next 6 sts, sc in last dc on Outer Ear; finish off leaving a long end for sewing.

Fold sts at end of Outer Ear to meet at the front and sew to the Head.

Torso

Rnd 1 (Right side)**:** With Brown, make an adjustable loop to form a ring; work 6 sc in ring; do **not** join, place marker.

Rnd 2: 2 Sc in each sc around: 12 sc.

Rnd 3: (Sc in next sc, 2 sc in next sc) around: 18 sc.

Rnd 4: (Sc in next 2 sc, 2 sc in next sc) around: 24 sc.

Rnd 5: (Sc in next 3 sc, 2 sc in next sc) around: 30 sc.

Rnd 6: (Sc in next 4 sc, 2 sc in next sc) around: 36 sc.

Rnds 7-13: Sc in each sc around.

Rnd 14: (Sc2tog, sc in next 4 sc) around: 30 sc.

Rnd 15: (Sc2tog, sc in next 3 sc) around; slip st in next sc, finish off leaving a long end for sewing: 24 sc.

Rear

Work same as Torso through Rnd 6: 36 sc.

Rnds 7-17: Sc in each sc around.

Rnd 18: (Sc2tog, sc in next 4 sc) around: 30 sc.

Rnd 19: Sc in each sc around; slip st in next sc, finish off leaving a long end for sewing.

Stuff Torso and Rear with polyester fiberfill.

With Neck at an angle, place Torso over Neck and sew in place.

With Torso at an angle, place Rear over Torso and sew in place.

With Off White, embroider spots on Torso and Back, using satin stitch *(Fig. 8b, page 47)*.

Tail

Rnd 1 (Right side)**:** With Brown, make an adjustable loop to form a ring; work 6 sc in ring; do **not** join, place marker.

Rnds 2 and 3: Sc in each sc around.

Rnd 4: (Sc in next sc, 2 sc in next sc) around: 9 sc.

Rnd 5: (Sc2tog, sc in next sc) around: 6 sc.

Rnd 6: Sc2tog around; slip st in next sc, finish off leaving a long end for sewing.

Flatten Tail and sew last rnd to Rnd 6 of Rear.

UNDERSIDE

With White, ch 3, (dc, hdc, 3 dc, hdc, dc, sc) in third ch from hook; join with slip st to top of beginning ch-3, finish off leaving a long end for sewing.

Sew Underside to Tail placing joining at beginning end of Tail.

Front Leg (Make 2)
UPPER LEG

Rnd 1 (Right side)**:** With Brown, make an adjustable loop to form a ring; work 6 sc in ring; do **not** join, place marker.

Rnd 2: 2 Sc in each sc around: 12 sc.

Rnd 3: (Sc in next sc, 2 sc in next sc) around: 18 sc.

Rnd 4: Sc in each sc around; slip st in next sc, finish off leaving a long end for sewing.

MID LEG

Rnd 1 (Right side)**:** With Brown, make an adjustable loop to form a ring; work 6 sc in ring; do **not** join, place marker.

Rnd 2: (Sc in next sc, 2 sc in next sc) around: 9 sc.

Rnds 3-9: Sc in each sc around.

Rnd 10: (Sc in next 2 sc, 2 sc in next sc) around; slip st in next sc, finish off leaving a long end for sewing: 12 sc.

LOWER LEG

Rnd 1 (Right side)**:** With Tan, make an adjustable loop to form a ring; work 4 sc in ring; do **not** join, place marker.

Rnd 2: 2 Sc in each sc around: 8 sc.

Rnds 3-6: Sc in each sc around.

Rnd 7: Sc in each sc around changing to Brown in last sc *(Fig. 4a, page 46)*; cut Tan.

Rnds 8-10: Sc in each sc around.

Slip st in next sc, finish off leaving a long end for sewing.

HOOF

Toe (Make 2)

Rnd 1 (Right side): With Black, make an adjustable loop to form a ring; work 4 sc in ring; do **not** join, place marker.

Rnd 2: Sc in each sc around; finish off leaving a long end for sewing.

Foot

Rnd 1: With **right** side facing, join Tan with slip st in any sc on Toe; ch 1, sc in same st and in next 2 sc, sc in each sc on second Toe; sc in last sc on first Toe; join with slip st to first sc, finish off leaving a long end for sewing.

Sew Toes together.

FRONT LEG ASSEMBLY

Sew Upper Leg to Torso.

Stuff both Leg pieces firmly with polyester fiberfill.

Sew Mid Leg to Upper Leg and Lower Leg to Mid Leg, adding additional stuffing until they are stiff enough to hold up the body weight.

Sew Hoof to Lower Leg.

Back Leg (Make 2)
UPPER LEG

Rnd 1 (Right side): With Brown, make an adjustable loop to form a ring; work 6 sc in ring; do **not** join, place marker.

Rnd 2: (Sc in next sc, 2 sc in next sc) around: 9 sc.

Rnds 3-6: Sc in each sc around.

Rnd 7: (Sc in next 2 sc, 2 sc in next sc) around: 12 sc.

Rnds 8-10: Sc in each sc around.

Slip st in next sc, finish off leaving a long end for sewing.

LOWER LEG

Rnd 1 (Right side): With Tan, make an adjustable loop to form a ring; work 4 sc in ring; do **not** join, place marker.

Rnd 2: 2 Sc in each sc around: 8 sc.

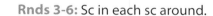

Rnds 3-6: Sc in each sc around.

Rnd 7: Sc in each sc around changing to Brown in last sc; cut Tan.

Rnds 8-11: Sc in each sc around.

Slip st in next sc, finish off leaving a long end for sewing.

HOOF

Work same as Front Leg.

BACK LEG ASSEMBLY

Stuff all Leg pieces firmly with polyester fiberfill.

Sew Upper Leg to Rear and Lower Leg to Upper Leg placing it at an angle, and adding additional stuffing until they are stiff enough to hold up the body weight.

Sew Hoof to Lower Leg.

Fox

EASY +

Finished Size: Approximately
5¾" tall (excluding ears) x 8½" long (14.5 cm x 21.5 cm)
Shown on page 8.

SHOPPING LIST

Yarn (Medium Weight)

☐ Orange - 155 yards (142 meters)
☐ Black - 40 yards (36.5 meters)
☐ Off White - 30 yards
   (27.5 meters)

Crochet Hook

☐ Size G (4 mm)

Additional Supplies

☐ Yarn needle
☐ Polyester fiberfill
☐ 12 mm Copper safety eyes - 2
   (Please take caution if the
   toy is for a child that is at
   risk of choking. See Safety,
   page 45.)

GAUGE INFORMATION

Gauge is **not** of great importance as
long as your crochet fabric is very
dense *(see Gauge, page 44)*.

——— STITCH GUIDE ———

TREBLE CROCHET *(abbreviated tr)*
YO twice, insert hook in st indicated,
YO and pull up a loop (4 loops on
hook), (YO and draw through 2 loops
on hook) 3 times.
SINGLE CROCHET 2 TOGETHER
   (abbreviated sc2tog)
Pull up a loop in each of next 2 sc, YO
and draw through all 3 loops on hook
(**counts as one sc**).

Head

Rnd 1 (Right side)**:** With Orange,
make an adjustable loop to form a
ring *(Figs. 1a-d, page 45)*; work 6 sc
in ring; do **not** join, place marker
to indicate beginning of rnd *(see
Markers, page 45)*.

Rnd 2: 2 Sc in each sc around: 12 sc.

Rnd 3: (Sc in next sc, 2 sc in next sc)
around: 18 sc.

Rnd 4: (Sc in next 2 sc, 2 sc in next sc)
around: 24 sc.

Rnd 5: (Sc in next 3 sc, 2 sc in next sc)
around: 30 sc.

Rnds 6-11: Sc in each sc around.

Rnd 12: (Sc2tog, sc in next 3 sc)
around changing to Off White in last
sc *(Fig. 4a, page 46)*; cut Orange:
24 sc.

Rnd 13: (Sc2tog, sc in next 2 sc)
around: 18 sc.

Attach safety eyes to Head, placing
them on Rnd 10 and spacing them
approximately 6 sc apart.

Stuff Head with polyester fiberfill.

Rnd 14: (Sc2tog, sc in next sc) around:
12 sc.

Rnd 15: Sc2tog around: 6 sc.

Continue to sc2tog around until hole
is closed; slip st in next sc, finish off.

Nose

Row 1 (Right side)**:** With Black, ch 4,
(dc, ch 3, slip st) in fourth ch from
hook; finish off leaving a long end for
sewing.

Muzzle

Rnd 1 (Right side)**:** With Orange,
make an adjustable loop to form a
ring; work 6 sc in ring; do **not** join,
place marker.

7

Rnd 2: 2 Sc in each sc around: 12 sc.

Rnds 3-6: Sc in each sc around.

Rnd 7: (Sc in next sc, 2 sc in next sc) around; slip st in next sc, finish off leaving a long end for sewing: 18 sc.

Upper Jaw (Make 2)
Row 1: With Off White, ch 3, 6 dc in third ch from hook.

Row 2 (Right side)**:** Ch 1, turn; 2 sc in each dc across; finish off leaving a long end for sewing: 12 sc.

Lower Jaw
Rnd 1 (Right side)**:** With Off White, ch 3, 11 dc in third ch from hook; join with slip st to top of beginning ch-3, finish off leaving a long end for sewing.

Head Assembly
Eyelid (Make 4)**:** With Orange, ch 4; finish off leaving a long end for sewing.

Use photos as guides for placement of all pieces. See Tips, page 45.

Sew Eyelids to Head above the safety eyes.

Use whipstitch *(Figs. 5a & b, page 46)* for the method of sewing to join the pieces together.

Sew Muzzle to Head, stuffing with polyester fiberfill.

Sew Lower Jaw to Muzzle leaving a space under the Nose for the Upper Jaws.

Sew Upper Jaws to Muzzle with edges touching under the Nose and overlapping the Lower Jaw, lightly stuffing with polyester fiberfill.

Sew Nose to Muzzle.

With Black, embroider a line from the Nose between the Upper Jaws, and curving along the bottom of the Upper Jaws using backstitch *(Fig. 6, page 46)*.

Ear (Make 2)
INNER EAR
With Off White, ch 4.

Row 1: (Sc, dc) in second ch from hook, (tr, ch 2, tr) in next ch, (dc, sc) in last ch: 6 sts and 1 ch-2 sp.

Row 2 (Right side)**:** Ch 1, turn; sc in first 3 sts, (sc, ch 2, sc) in next ch-2 sp, sc in last 3 sts; finish off leaving a long end for sewing: 8 sc and 1 ch-2 sp.

Note: Loop a short piece of yarn around any stitch to mark Row 2 as **right** side.

OUTER EAR
Using Black, work same as Inner Ear; do **not** finish off: 8 sc and 1 ch-2 sp.

Joining Row: Ch 1, turn; holding Inner Ear in front of Outer Ear, with **wrong** sides together, matching sts, and working through **both** loops on **both** pieces, sc in first 4 sc, (sc, ch 2, sc) in next ch-2 sp, sc in last 4 sc; finish off leaving a long end for sewing.

Sew Ears to Head, slightly curving bottom edges.

Belly

With Off White, ch 21.

Row 1: Dc in third ch from hook and in next 17 chs, 5 dc in last ch; working in free loops of beginning ch *(Fig. 3b, page 46)*, dc in next 18 chs; do **not** join: 41 dc.

Row 2 (Right side)**:** Ch 2, turn; dc in first 19 dc, 2 dc in each of next 3 dc, dc in each dc across; finish off leaving a long end for sewing.

Note: Mark Row 2 as **right** side.

Torso

Rnd 1 (Right side)**:** With Orange, make an adjustable loop to form a ring; work 6 sc in ring; do **not** join, place marker.

Rnd 2: 2 Sc in each sc around: 12 sc.

Rnd 3: (Sc in next sc, 2 sc in next sc) around: 18 sc.

Rnd 4: (Sc in next 2 sc, 2 sc in next sc) around: 24 sc.

Rnd 5: (Sc in next 3 sc, 2 sc in next sc) around: 30 sc.

Rnd 6: (Sc in next 4 sc, 2 sc in next sc) around: 36 sc.

Rnds 7-12: Sc in each sc around.

Rnd 13: (Sc2tog, sc in next 4 sc) around: 30 sc.

Rnd 14: Sc in each sc around.

Rnd 15: (Sc2tog, sc in next 3 sc) around; slip st in next sc, finish off leaving a long end for sewing: 24 sc.

Rear

Work same as Torso through Rnd 13: 30 sc.

Rnds 14-18: Sc in each sc around.

Slip st in next sc, finish off leaving a long end for sewing.

Stuff Torso and Rear with polyester fiberfill.

With Head at an angle, place Torso over Head and sew in place.

Place Rear over Torso and sew in place.

Placing straight edge of Belly at neck, sew Belly to the underside of the body.

Tail

BASE

Rnd 1 (Right side)**:** With Orange, make an adjustable loop to form a ring; work 6 sc in ring; do **not** join, place marker.

Rnd 2: 2 Sc in each sc around: 12 sc.

Rnd 3: (Sc in next sc, 2 sc in next sc) around: 18 sc.

Rnd 4: Sc in each sc around.

Rnd 5: Sc2tog 6 times, sc in next 6 sc: 12 sc.

Rnd 6: Sc in each sc around.

Stuff Base with polyester fiberfill.

Rnd 7: Sc2tog 4 times, slip st in next sc, leave remaining 3 sts unworked; finish off leaving a long end for sewing.

Sew Base to Rear.

MIDDLE

Work same as Base, page 9, through Rnd 3: 18 sc.

Rnd 4: Sc in each sc around.

Rnd 5: Sc2tog 6 times, 2 sc in each of next 6 sc: 18 sc.

Rnds 6 and 7: Repeat Rnds 4 and 5.

Rnds 8-11: Sc in each sc around.

Rnd 12: Sc2tog 6 times, 2 sc in each of next 6 sc: 18 sc.

Rnd 13: Sc in each sc around; slip st in next sc, finish off leaving a long end for sewing.

Stuff Middle with polyester fiberfill, then sew to the side of Base to form a curve.

TIP

Rnd 1 (Right side)**:** With Off White, make an adjustable loop to form a ring; work 6 sc in ring; do **not** join, place marker.

Rnd 2: (Sc in next sc, 2 sc in next sc) around: 9 sc.

Rnd 3: Sc in each sc around.

Rnd 4: (Sc in next 2 sc, 2 sc in next sc) around: 12 sc.

Rnd 5: (Sc in next 3 sc, 2 sc in next sc) around changing to Dark Orange in last sc made; cut Off White: 15 sc.

Rnds 6 and 7: Sc in each sc around.

Slip st in next sc, finish off leaving a long end for sewing.

Stuff Tip with polyester fiberfill, then sew to side of Middle to form a curve.

Front Leg (Make 2)
UPPER LEG

Rnd 1 (Right side)**:** With Orange, make an adjustable loop to form a ring; work 6 sc in ring; do **not** join, place marker.

Rnd 2: 2 Sc in each sc around: 12 sc.

Rnd 3: Sc in each sc around; slip st in next sc, finish off leaving a long end for sewing.

LOWER LEG

Rnd 1 (Right side)**:** With Black, make an adjustable loop to form a ring; work 6 sc in ring; do **not** join, place marker.

Rnd 2: (Sc in next sc, 2 sc in next sc) around: 9 sc.

Rnds 3-6: Sc in each sc around.

Rnd 7: (Sc in next 2 sc, 2 sc in next sc) around: 12 sc.

Rnd 8: Sc in each sc around.

Rnd 9: Sc in each sc around changing to Orange in last sc; cut Black.

Rnds 10 and 11: Sc in each sc around.

Slip st in next sc, finish off leaving a long end for sewing.

PAW
Rnd 1 (Right side)**:** With Black, make an adjustable loop to form a ring; work 6 sc in ring; do **not** join, place marker.

Rnd 2: Sc in each sc around.

Rnd 3: (Sc in next 2 sc, 3 sc in next sc) twice; slip st in next sc, finish off leaving a long end for sewing: 10 sc.

FRONT LEG ASSEMBLY
Stuff all 3 Leg pieces firmly with polyester fiberfill.

Sew Upper Leg to Torso overlapping edge of Belly. Sew Lower Leg to Upper Leg, adding additional stuffing until they are stiff enough to hold up the body weight.

Sew Paw to side of Lower Leg.

With Black, embroider 2 toes on each Paw using straight stitches (*Fig. 7, page 46*).

Back Leg (Make 2)
UPPER LEG
Rnd 1 (Right side)**:** With Orange, make an adjustable loop to form a ring; work 6 sc in ring; do **not** join, place marker.

Rnd 2: 2 Sc in each sc around: 12 sc.

Rnd 3: (Sc in next sc, 2 sc in next sc) around: 18 sc.

Rnd 4: (Sc in next 2 sc, 2 sc in next sc) around: 24 sc.

Rnd 5: Sc in each sc around; slip st in next sc, finish off leaving a long end for sewing.

MID LEG
Rnd 1 (Right side)**:** With Orange, ch 3, sc in second ch from hook, 3 sc in last ch; working in free loop of beginning ch, 2 sc in next ch; do **not** join, place marker: 6 sc.

Rnd 2: (Sc in next 2 sc, 3 sc in next sc) twice: 10 sc.

Rnd 3: Sc in each sc around.

Rnd 4: ★ Sc in next 2 sc, 2 sc in next sc, sc in next sc, 2 sc in next sc; repeat from ★ once **more**; slip st in next sc, finish off leaving a long end for sewing: 14 sc.

LOWER LEG
Rnd 1 (Right side)**:** With Black, make an adjustable loop to form a ring; work 6 sc in ring; do **not** join, place marker.

Rnd 2: (Sc in next 2 sc, 3 sc in next sc) twice: 10 sc.

Rnd 3: ★ Sc in next 2 sc, 2 sc in next sc, sc in next sc, 2 sc in next sc; repeat from ★ once **more**; slip st in next sc, finish off leaving a long end for sewing: 14 sc.

PAW
Rnd 1 (Right side)**:** With Black, make an adjustable loop to form a ring; work 6 sc in ring; do **not** join, place marker.

Rnd 2: Sc in each sc around.

Rnd 3: (Sc in next 2 sc, 3 sc in next sc) twice: 10 sc.

Rnds 4-9: Sc in each sc around.

Slip st in next sc, finish off leaving a long end for sewing.

BACK LEG ASSEMBLY
Stuff all 4 Leg pieces firmly with polyester fiberfill.

Sew Upper Leg to Rear. Sew Mid Leg to side of Upper Leg facing forward. Sew Lower Leg to side of Upper Leg under Mid Leg slightly overlapping edge of Belly. Sew Paw to side of Lower Leg.

With Black, embroider 2 toes on each Paw using straight stitches.

Rabbit

 EASY +

Finished Size: Approximately 4¹/₂"
tall (excluding ears) x 8¹/₂" long (11.5 cm x 21.5 cm)

SHOPPING LIST

Yarn (Medium Weight) 🧶 **4 MEDIUM**

- ☐ Light Brown - 245 yards (224 meters)
- ☐ Off White - 36 yards (33 meters)
- ☐ Pink - 12 yards (11 meters)
- ☐ Dark Brown - small amount

Crochet Hook

- ☐ Size G (4 mm)

Additional Supplies

- ☐ Yarn needle
- ☐ Polyester fiberfill
- ☐ Pink embroidery floss
- ☐ 12 mm Brown safety eyes - 2 (Please take caution if the toy is for a child that is at risk of choking. See Safety, page 45.)

GAUGE INFORMATION

Gauge is **not** of great importance as long as your crochet fabric is very dense *(see Gauge, page 44)*.

——— STITCH GUIDE ———

SINGLE CROCHET 2 TOGETHER
(abbreviated sc2tog)

Pull up a loop in each of next 2 sc, YO and draw through all 3 loops on hook (**counts as one sc**).

Head

Rnd 1 (Right side)**:** With Light Brown, make an adjustable loop to form a ring *(Figs. 1a-d, page 45)*; work 6 sc in ring; do **not** join, place marker to indicate beginning of rnd *(see Markers, page 45)*.

Rnd 2: 2 Sc in each sc around: 12 sc.

Rnd 3: (Sc in next sc, 2 sc in next sc) around: 18 sc.

Rnds 4-6: Sc in each sc around.

Rnd 7: (Sc in next 2 sc, 2 sc in next sc) around: 24 sc.

Rnds 8-10: Sc in each sc around.

Rnd 11: (Sc in next 3 sc, 2 sc in next sc) around: 30 sc.

Rnds 12-16: Sc in each sc around.

Rnd 17: (Sc2tog, sc in next 3 sc) around: 24 sc.

Rnd 18: (Sc2tog, sc in next 2 sc) around: 18 sc.

Attach safety eyes to Head, placing them on Rnd 9 and spacing them approximately 8 sc apart.

Stuff Head with polyester fiberfill.

Rnd 19: (Sc2tog, sc in next sc) around: 12 sc.

Rnd 20: Sc2tog around: 6 sc.

Continue to sc2tog around until hole is closed; slip st in next sc, finish off.

Cheek (Make 2)

Rnd 1 (Right side): With Light Brown, make an adjustable loop to form a ring; work 6 sc in ring; do **not** join, place marker.

Rnd 2: (Sc in next 2 sc, 3 sc in next sc) twice: 10 sc.

Rnd 3: ★ Sc in next 2 sc, 2 sc in next sc, sc in next sc, 2 sc in next sc; repeat from ★ once **more**: 14 sc.

Rnd 4: Sc in next 3 sc, 2 sc in next sc, sc in next sc, 2 sc in next sc, sc in next 4 sc, 2 sc in next sc, sc in next 2 sc changing to Off White in last sc *(Fig. 4a, page 46)*; cut Light Brown leaving a long end for sewing, remove marker, sc in next 5 sc, slip st in next sc; finish off leaving a long end for sewing.

Nose

Rnd 1 (Right side): With Pink, make an adjustable loop to form a ring; work 4 sc in ring changing to Light Brown in last sc made, cut Pink leaving a long end for sewing, 4 dc in ring; join with slip st to first sc, finish off leaving a long end for sewing.

Upper Jaw (Make 2)

Rnd 1 (Right side): With Light Brown, ch 3, 12 dc in third ch from hook; join with slip st to top of beginning ch-3, finish off leaving a long end for sewing.

Lower Jaw

Rnd 1 (Right side): With Light Brown, ch 3, 11 dc in third ch from hook; join with slip st to top of beginning ch-3, finish off leaving a long end for sewing.

Head Assembly

Eyelid (Make 4): With Off White, ch 7 tightly; finish off leaving a long end for sewing.

Inner Eyelid (Make 2): With Pink floss, ch 10 tightly; finish off leaving a long end for sewing.

Use photos as guides for placement of all pieces. See Tips, page 45.

Sew Inner Eyelid under the safety eyes. Sew one Eyelid over the safety eye. Sew one Eyelid under the Inner Eyelid, from inner eye to top of upper Eyelid.

Use whipstitch *(Figs. 5a & b, page 46)* for the method of sewing to join the pieces together.

Using matching color, sew Nose to Head. Pinch the area between the eyes together to form a bridge and make a couple of stitches from side to side near the inner eyes to hold it in place.

Sew Lower Jaw to Head leaving a space under the Nose for the Upper Jaws.

Sew Upper Jaws to Head with edges touching under the Nose and overlapping the Lower Jaw, lightly stuffing with polyester fiberfill.

Sew Cheeks to Head next to Upper Jaws with Off White area to the bottom and stuffing lightly with polyester fiberfill.

With Dark Brown, embroider a line from the Nose between the Upper Jaws, and curving along the bottom of the Upper Jaws using backstitch *(Fig. 6, page 46)*.

Ear (Make 2)
INNER EAR
With Pink, ch 9.

Rnd 1 (Right side)**:** Sc in second ch from hook and in next 6 chs, 3 sc in last ch; working in free loops of beginning ch *(Fig. 3b, page 46)*, sc in next 6 chs, 2 sc in next ch; join with slip st to first sc: 18 sc.

Note: Loop a short piece of yarn around any stitch to mark Rnd 1 as **right** side.

Rnd 2: Ch 1, 2 sc in same sc as joining, sc in next 6 sc, 2 sc in next sc, sc in next sc, 2 sc in next sc, sc in next 6 sc, 2 sc in next sc, sc in last sc; cut Pink, with Off White, join with slip st to first sc *(Fig. 4b, page 46)*: 22 sc.

Rnd 3: Ch 1, 2 sc in same sc as joining, sc in next 8 sc, 2 sc in next sc, sc in next sc, 2 sc in next sc, sc in next 8 sc, 2 sc in next sc, sc in last sc; join with slip st to first sc, finish off: 26 sc.

OUTER EAR
With Light Brown, ch 9.

Rnd 1 (Right side)**:** Sc in second ch from hook and in next 6 chs, 3 sc in last ch; working in free loops of beginning ch, sc in next 6 chs, 2 sc in next ch; join with slip st to first sc: 18 sc.

Note: Mark Rnd 1 as **right** side.

Rnd 2: Ch 1, 2 sc in same sc as joining, sc in next 6 sc, 2 sc in next sc, sc in next sc, 2 sc in next sc, sc in next 6 sc, 2 sc in next sc, sc in last sc; join with slip st to first sc: 22 sc.

Rnd 3: Ch 1, 2 sc in same sc as joining, sc in next 8 sc, 2 sc in next sc, sc in next sc, 2 sc in next sc, sc in next 8 sc, 2 sc in next sc, sc in last sc; join with slip st to first sc: 26 sc.

Joining Rnd: Ch 1, turn; holding Inner Ear in front of Outer Ear, with **wrong** sides together, and working through **both** loops on **both** pieces, sc in each sc around; join with slip st to first sc, finish off leaving a long end for sewing.

Fold one end of Ears in half and sew to Head with Outer Ears toward center.

Belly

With Off White, ch 21.

Row 1: Dc in third ch from hook and in next 17 chs, 5 dc in last ch; working in free loops of beginning ch, dc in next 18 chs; do **not** join: 41 dc.

Row 2 (Right side)**:** Ch 2, turn; dc in first 19 dc, 2 dc in each of next 3 dc, dc in each dc across; finish off leaving a long end for sewing.

Note: Mark Row 2 as **right** side.

Torso

Rnd 1 (Right side)**:** With Light Brown, make an adjustable loop to form a ring; work 6 sc in ring; do **not** join, place marker.

Rnd 2: 2 Sc in each sc around: 12 sc.

Rnd 3: (Sc in next sc, 2 sc in next sc) around: 18 sc.

Rnd 4: (Sc in next 2 sc, 2 sc in next sc) around: 24 sc.

Rnd 5: (Sc in next 3 sc, 2 sc in next sc) around: 30 sc.

Rnd 6: (Sc in next 4 sc, 2 sc in next sc) around: 36 sc.

Rnd 7: (Sc in next 5 sc, 2 sc in next sc) around: 42 sc.

Rnds 8-13: Sc in each sc around.

Rnd 14: (Sc2tog, sc in next 5 sc) around: 36 sc.

Rnd 15: (Sc2tog, sc in next 4 sc) around: 30 sc.

Rnd 16: (Sc2tog, sc in next 3 sc) around; slip st in next sc, finish off leaving a long end for sewing: 24 sc.

Mid Section

Work same as Torso through Rnd 7: 42 sc.

Rnds 8-10: Sc in each sc around.

Slip st in next sc, finish off leaving a long end for sewing.

Rear

Work same as Torso through Rnd 7: 42 sc.

Rnd 8: (Sc in next 6 sc, 2 sc in next sc) around: 48 sc.

Rnd 9: (Sc in next 7 sc, 2 sc in next sc) around: 54 sc.

Rnds 10-17: Sc in each sc around.

Rnd 18: (Sc2tog, sc in next 7 sc) around: 48 sc.

Rnds 19 and 20: Sc in each sc around.

Rnd 21: (Sc2tog, sc in next 6 sc) around: 42 sc.

Rnds 22 and 23: Sc in each sc around.

Rnd 24: (Sc2tog, sc in next 5 sc) around: 36 sc.

Rnd 25: Sc in each sc around; slip st in next sc, finish off leaving a long end for sewing.

Stuff Torso, Mid Section, and Rear with polyester fiberfill.

With Head at an angle, place Torso over Head and sew in place.

Place Mid Section over Torso and sew in place.

Place Rear over Mid Section and sew in place.

Placing straight edge of Belly at neck, sew Belly to the underside of the body.

Tail

Rnd 1 (Right side)**:** With Off White, make an adjustable loop to form a ring; work 6 sc in ring; do **not** join, place marker.

Rnd 2: 2 Sc in each sc around: 12 sc.

Rnd 3: (Sc in next sc, 2 sc in next sc) around: 18 sc.

Rnd 4: Sc in each sc around changing to Light Brown in last sc; cut Off White.

Rnd 5: Sc in next 10 sc, sc2tog 4 times: 14 sc.

Rnd 6: Sc in next 10 sc, sc2tog twice; slip st in next sc, finish off leaving a long end for sewing.

Stuff Tail with polyester fiberfill, then sew to Rear with decreases towards the top.

Front Leg (Make 2)
UPPER LEG
Rnd 1 (Right side)**:** With Light Brown, make an adjustable loop to form a ring; work 6 sc in ring; do **not** join, place marker.

Rnd 2: 2 Sc in each sc around: 12 sc.

Rnd 3: (Sc in next sc, 2 sc in next sc) around: 18 sc.

Rnd 4: Sc in each sc around; slip st in next sc, finish off leaving a long end for sewing.

LOWER LEG
With Off White, work same as Upper Leg through Rnd 2: 12 sc.

Rnd 3: Sc in each sc around changing to Light Brown in last sc; cut Off White.

Rnds 4-6: Sc in each sc around.

Slip st in next sc, finish off leaving a long end for sewing.

PAW
Rnd 1 (Right side)**:** With Off White, make an adjustable loop to form a ring; work 6 sc in ring; do **not** join, place marker.

Rnd 2: Sc in each sc around.

Rnd 3: (Sc in next 2 sc, 3 sc in next sc) twice; slip st in next sc, finish off leaving a long end for sewing: 10 sc.

FRONT LEG ASSEMBLY
Stuff all 3 Leg pieces firmly with polyester fiberfill.

Sew Upper Leg to Torso overlapping edge of Belly. Sew Lower Leg to Upper Leg, adding additional stuffing until they are stiff enough to hold up the body weight.

Sew Paw on Lower Leg.

With Dark Brown, embroider 3 toes on each Paw using straight stitches *(Fig. 7, page 46)*.

Back Leg (Make 2)

UPPER LEG

Rnd 1 (Right side)**:** With Light Brown, make an adjustable loop to form a ring; work 6 sc in ring; do **not** join, place marker.

Rnd 2: 2 Sc in each sc around: 12 sc.

Rnd 3: (Sc in next 2 sc, 2 sc in each of next 4 sc) twice: 20 sc.

Rnd 4: Sc in each sc around.

Rnd 5: (Sc in next 2 sc, 2 sc in each of next 2 sc) twice, sc in next 4 sc, (2 sc in each of next 2 sc, sc in next 2 sc) twice: 28 sc.

Rnd 6: Sc in next 5 sc, 2 sc in each of next 4 sc, sc in next 10 sc, 2 sc in each of next 4 sc, sc in next 5 sc: 36 sc.

Rnd 7: Sc in each sc around; slip st in next sc, finish off leaving a long end for sewing.

LOWER LEG

Rnd 1 (Right side)**:** With Light Brown, make an adjustable loop to form a ring; work 6 sc in ring; do **not** join, place marker.

Rnd 2: 2 Sc in each sc around: 12 sc.

Rnds 3-5: Sc in each sc around.

Slip st in next sc, finish off leaving a long end for sewing.

PAW

Rnd 1 (Right side)**:** With Off White, make an adjustable loop to form a ring; work 6 sc in ring; do **not** join, place marker.

Rnd 2: Sc in each sc around.

Rnd 3: (Sc in next 2 sc, 3 sc in next sc) twice: 10 sc.

Rnd 4: Sc in each sc around changing to Light Brown in last sc; cut Off White.

Rnds 5-9: Sc in each sc around.

Slip st in next sc, finish off leaving a long end for sewing.

BACK LEG ASSEMBLY

Stuff all 3 Leg pieces firmly with polyester fiberfill.

Sew Upper Leg to Rear. Sew Lower Leg to Upper Leg, adding additional stuffing until they are stiff enough to hold the body weight.

Sew Paw on Lower Leg.

With Dark Brown, embroider 3 toes on each Paw using straight stitches.

Baby Owl

EASY +

Finished Size: Approximately 3" (7.5 cm) tall

SHOPPING LIST

Yarn (Medium Weight)

- ☐ Dark Brown - 46 yards (42 meters)
- ☐ Brown - small amount
- ☐ Grey - small amount

Crochet Hook

- ☐ Size G (4 mm)

Additional Supplies

- ☐ Yarn needle
- ☐ Polyester fiberfill
- ☐ 10.5 mm Yellow safety eyes - 2 (Please take caution if the toy is for a child that is at risk of choking. See Safety, page 45.)

GAUGE INFORMATION

Gauge is **not** of great importance as long as your crochet fabric is very dense (*see Gauge, page 44*).

─── STITCH GUIDE ───

SINGLE CROCHET 2 TOGETHER
(abbreviated sc2tog)

Pull up a loop in each of next 2 sc, YO and draw through all 3 loops on hook (**counts as one sc**).

Face

Rnd 1 (Right side): With Brown, make an adjustable loop to form a ring *(Figs. 1a-d, page 45)*; work 6 sc in ring; do **not** join, place marker to indicate beginning of rnd (*see Markers, page 45*).

Rnd 2: 2 Sc in each sc around: 12 sc.

Rnd 3: Skip next sc, 5 dc in next sc, skip next sc, sc in next 2 sc, (sc, ch 2, sc) in next sc, sc in next 2 sc, skip next sc, 5 dc in next sc, skip next sc, slip st in next sc; finish off leaving a long end for sewing.

Using Dark Brown, work same as Face for 2 Wings and a Tail.

Body

Rnd 1 (Right side): With Dark Brown, make an adjustable loop to form a ring; work 6 sc in ring; do **not** join, place marker.

Rnd 2: 2 Sc in each sc around: 12 sc.

Rnd 3: (Sc in next sc, 2 sc in next sc) around: 18 sc.

Rnd 4: (Sc in next 2 sc, 2 sc in next sc) around: 24 sc.

Rnd 5: (Sc in next 3 sc, 2 sc in next sc) around: 30 sc.

Rnds 6-9: Sc in each sc around.

Rnd 10: (Sc in next 4 sc, 2 sc in next sc) around: 36 sc.

Rnds 11-14: Sc in each sc around.

Rnd 15: (Sc2tog, sc in next 4 sc) around: 30 sc.

Rnd 16: (Sc2tog, sc in next 3 sc) around: 24 sc.

Rnd 17: (Sc2tog, sc in next 2 sc) around: 18 sc.

Use photos as guides for placement of all pieces. See Tips, page 45.

Insert the safety eyes through the base of each 5-dc group on Rnd 3 of the Face, then through Rnd 8 of the Body with the point of the Face toward the last rnd worked.

Stuff Body with polyester fiberfill.

Rnd 18: (Sc2tog, sc in next sc) around: 12 sc.

Rnd 19: Sc2tog around: 6 sc.

Continue to sc2tog around until hole is closed; slip st in next sc, finish off.

Use whipstitch *(Figs. 5a & b, page 46)* for the method of sewing to join the pieces together.

Sew the Face in place.

Sew the top of the heart shape of the Wings to Rnd 7 of the Body with the point toward the last rnd worked.

Sew the point of the Tail to Rnd 12 of the Body.

Beak

BOTTOM

With Grey, make an adjustable loop to form a ring; work 6 sc in ring; join with slip st to first sc, finish off leaving a long end for sewing.

TOP

With Grey, make an adjustable loop to form a ring; work (2 sc, ch 2, 2 sc) in ring; do **not** join, finish off leaving a long end for sewing.

Sew the Bottom Beak to the Face near the point. Sew the straight edge of the Top Beak above the Bottom Beak.

Foot (Make 2)

Rnd 1 (Right side)**:** With Grey, make an adjustable loop to form a ring; work 6 sc in ring; do **not** join.

Rnd 2: † Ch 5, sc in second ch from hook and in last 3 chs (toe made), sc in next sc, ch 5, sc in second ch from hook and in last 3 chs (toe made) †, sc in next 2 sc, repeat from † to † once, sc in next sc, slip st in last sc; finish off leaving a long end for sewing.

Fold each toe and whipstitch across to form skinny pieces, then sew the center of each Foot to the bottom of the Body.

Great Horned Owl

■■□□ **EASY +**

Finished Size: Approximately 5" (12.5 cm) tall

SHOPPING LIST

Yarn (Medium Weight)

- ☐ Multi - 140 yards (128 meters)
- ☐ Off White - small amount
- ☐ Black - small amount
- ☐ Tan - small amount

Crochet Hook

- ☐ Size G (4 mm)

Additional Supplies

- ☐ Yarn needle
- ☐ Polyester fiberfill
- ☐ 12 mm Yellow safety eyes - 2 (Please take caution if the toy is for a child that is at risk of choking. See Safety, page 45.)

GAUGE INFORMATION

Gauge is **not** of great importance as long as your crochet fabric is very dense (*see Gauge, page 44*).

── STITCH GUIDE ──

TREBLE CROCHET (*abbreviated tr*)
YO twice, insert hook in st indicated, YO and pull up a loop (4 loops on hook), (YO and draw through 2 loops on hook) 3 times.

SINGLE CROCHET 2 TOGETHER
   (*abbreviated sc2tog*)
Pull up a loop in each of next 2 sc, YO and draw through all 3 loops on hook (**counts as one sc**).

Right Eye Patch

Rnd 1 (Right side)**:** With Tan, make an adjustable loop to form a ring (*Figs. 1a-d, page 45*); work 6 sc in ring; do **not** join, place marker to indicate beginning of rnd (*see Markers, page 45*).

Note: Loop a short piece of yarn around any stitch to mark Rnd 1 as **right** side.

Rnd 2: 2 Sc in each sc around: 12 sc.

Rnd 3: (Sc in next sc, 2 sc in next sc) around: 18 sc.

Rnd 4: (Sc in next 2 sc, 2 sc in next sc) around changing to Black in last sc made (*Fig. 4a, page 46*); cut Tan: 24 sc.

Rnd 5: (Sc in next 3 sc, 2 sc in next sc) 3 times changing to Off White in last sc made; cut Black, sc in next 4 sc, [skip next sc, (sc, dc, sc) in next sc] 3 times, skip next sc, slip st in next sc; finish off leaving a long end for sewing.

Left Eye Patch

Work same as Right Eye Patch through Rnd 4: 24 sc.

Rnd 5: (Sc in next 3 sc, 2 sc in next sc) 3 times changing to Off White in last sc made; cut Black, slip st in next sc, [skip next sc, (sc, dc, sc) in next sc] 3 times, skip next sc, sc in next 4 sc; finish off leaving a long end for sewing.

Body

Rnd 1 (Right side): With Multi, make an adjustable loop to form a ring; work 6 sc in ring; do **not** join, place marker.

Rnd 2: 2 Sc in each sc around: 12 sc.

Rnd 3: (Sc in next sc, 2 sc in next sc) around: 18 sc.

Rnd 4: (Sc in next 2 sc, 2 sc in next sc) around: 24 sc.

Rnd 5: (Sc in next 3 sc, 2 sc in next sc) around: 30 sc.

Rnd 6: (Sc in next 4 sc, 2 sc in next sc) around: 36 sc.

Rnds 7 and 8: Sc in each sc around.

Rnd 9: (Sc in next 5 sc, 2 sc in next sc) around: 42 sc.

Rnds 10 and 11: Sc in each sc around.

Rnd 12: (Sc in next 6 sc, 2 sc in next sc) around: 48 sc.

Rnds 13 and 14: Sc in each sc around.

Rnd 15: (Sc in next 7 sc, 2 sc in next sc) around: 54 sc.

Rnds 16 and 17: Sc in each sc around.

Rnd 18: (Sc in next 8 sc, 2 sc in next sc) around: 60 sc.

Rnds 19 and 20: Sc in each sc around.

Rnd 21: (Sc2tog, sc in next 8 sc) around: 54 sc.

Rnds 22 and 23: Sc in each sc around.

Rnd 24: (Sc2tog, sc in next 7 sc) around: 48 sc.

Rnds 25 and 26: Sc in each sc around.

Using photo as a guide for placement, insert the safety eyes through Rnd 2 of the Eye Patches, then through Rnd 10 of the Body, spacing the Patches approximately 2 sc apart.

Stuff Body with polyester fiberfill. Leave the remaining rounds unstuffed for a flat bottom.

Rnd 27: Working in Back Loops Only *(Fig. 2, page 45)*, (sc2tog, sc in next 6 sc) around: 42 sc.

Rnd 28: Working in Back Loops Only, (sc2tog, sc in next 5 sc) around: 36 sc.

Rnd 29: Working in both loops, (sc2tog, sc in next 4 sc) around: 30 sc.

Rnd 30: (Sc2tog, sc in next 3 sc) around: 24 sc.

Rnd 31: (Sc2tog, sc in next 2 sc) around: 18 sc.

Rnd 32: (Sc2tog, sc in next sc) around: 12 sc.

Rnd 33: Sc2tog around: 6 sc.

Continue to sc2tog around until hole is closed; slip st in next sc, finish off.

Face

Eyelid (Make 4)**:** With Off White, ch 5; finish off leaving a long end for sewing.

Use photos as guides for placement of all pieces. See Tips, page 45.

Sew Eyelids to Eye Patches above the safety eyes.

TOP BEAK
With Black, ch 6.

Row 1: Sc in second ch from hook, hdc in next ch, (dc, tr, ch 2, tr, dc) in next ch, hdc in next ch, sc in last ch; finish off leaving a long end for sewing.

BOTTOM BEAK

With Black, ch 6.

Row 1: Sc in second ch from hook, hdc in next ch, (dc, ch 2, dc) in next ch, hdc in next ch, sc in last ch; finish off leaving a long end for sewing.

Fold Bottom Beak in half at the ch-2 and sew across the top of the stitches.

Use whipstitch (*Figs. 5a & b, page 46*) for the method of sewing to join the pieces together.

Fold the Top Beak over the Bottom Beak and sew the Bottom Beak inside of the Top Beak.

Sew both pieces to the Body with the Off White on the Eye Patches overlapping the Beak.

Sew Eye Patches in place.

Right Ear Tuft

With Multi, ch 9.

Row 1 (Right side)**:** (Sc, hdc) in second ch from hook, dc in next 2 chs, tr in next 2 chs, dc in next ch, hdc in next ch, sc in last ch; finish off leaving a long end for sewing: 9 sts.

Row 2: With **right** side facing, join Black with slip st in first sc; ch 1, sc in same st and in next hdc, (sc, ch 3, sc) in next 5 sts, sc in next hdc, slip st in last sc; finish off.

Sew beginning ch of Right Ear Tuft to Body beginning at top of Right Eye Patch, curving edge downward.

Left Ear Tuft

With Multi, ch 9.

Row 1 (Right side)**:** Sc in second ch from hook, hdc in next ch, dc in next ch, tr in next 2 chs, dc in next 2 chs, (hdc, sc) in last ch; finish off leaving a long end for sewing: 9 sts.

Row 2: With **right** side facing, join Black with slip st in first sc; sc in next hdc, (sc, ch 3, sc) in next 5 sts, sc in last 2 sts; finish off.

Sew beginning ch of Left Ear Tuft to Body ending at top of Left Eye Patch, curving edge downward.

Wing (Make 2)

Rnd 1 (Right side)**:** With Multi, make an adjustable loop to form a ring; work 6 sc in ring; do **not** join, place marker.

Rnd 2: 2 Sc in each sc around: 12 sc.

Rnd 3: (Sc in next sc, 2 sc in next sc) around: 18 sc.

Rnd 4: (Sc in next 2 sc, 2 sc in next sc) around: 24 sc.

Rnd 5: (Sc in next 3 sc, 2 sc in next sc) around: 30 sc.

Begin working in rows.

Row 1: ★ Skip next sc, 5 dc in next sc, skip next sc, sc in next sc; repeat from ★ 3 times **more**, leave remaining 14 sc unworked.

Row 2: Turn; skip first sc, slip st in next 2 dc and from **front** to **back** around post of next dc (*Fig. A*), ★ skip next 2 dc, 5 dc in Front Loop Only of next sc, skip next 2 dc, slip st from **front** to **back** around post of next dc; repeat from ★ 2 times **more**, leave remaining sts unworked.

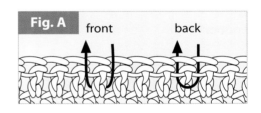

Fig. A front   back

Row 3: Turn; slip st in first 2 dc and from **back** to **front** around post of next dc, ★ skip next 2 dc, 5 dc in Back Loop Only of next slip st, skip next 2 dc, slip st from **back** to **front** around post of next dc; repeat from ★ once **more**, leave remaining sts unworked.

Row 4: Turn; slip st in next 2 dc and from **front** to **back** around post of next dc, skip next 2 dc, 5 dc in Front Loop Only of next slip st, skip next 2 dc, slip st from **front** to **back** around post of next dc and in last 2 dc; finish off.

Right Wing Edging: With **right** side facing, join Off White with slip st in first dc on Row 4; slip st in next 2 dc, sc in each st across previous rows and in next 7 sc of Rnd 5, slip st in next sc; finish off.

Left Wing Edging: With **right** side facing, skip 6 sc on Rnd 5 from end of Row 1 and join Off White with slip st in next sc, sc in next 7 sc, sc in each st across previous rows to last 3 dc on Row 4, slip st in next 3 dc; finish off.

Sew 6 unworked sts on Rnd 5 of the Wings to the Body.

Foot (Make 2)

Rnd 1 (Right side)**:** With Tan, make an adjustable loop to form a ring; work 6 sc in ring; do **not** join.

Rnd 2: Ch 5, sc in second ch from hook and in last 3 chs (toe made), ★ sc in next sc, ch 5, sc in second ch from hook and in last 3 chs (toe made); repeat from ★ once **more**, sc in next 2 sc, ch 3, sc in second ch from hook, slip st in last ch, leave remaining sc unworked; finish off leaving a long end for sewing.

Whipstitch across each toe to form skinny pieces, then sew the center of each Foot to the bottom of the Body.

With Black, embroider a line on each toe for talons using straight stitch *(Fig. 7, page 46)*.

Tail

With Multi, ch 9.

Row 1 (Right side)**:** Dc in third ch from hook and in next 5 chs, 5 dc in last ch; working in free loops of beginning ch *(Fig. 3b, page 46)*, dc in next 6 chs; do **not** join: 17 dc.

Note: Mark Row 1 as **right** side.

Row 2: Ch 3 (**counts as first dc**), turn; working in Front Loops Only, dc in next 3 dc, 4 dc in next dc, skip next dc, slip st from **front** to **back** around post of next 5 dc, skip next dc, working in Front Loops Only, 4 dc in next dc, dc in last 4 dc; finish off leaving a long end for sewing: 21 sts.

Row 3: With **right** side facing and working in Back Loops Only, skip first 4 dc and join Off White with slip st in next dc; sc in next 11 sts, slip st in next dc, leave remaining 4 dc unworked; finish off.

Sew end of rows on Tail to Rnd 25 of Body.

Fairy

EASY +

Finished Size: Approximately 7" (18 cm) tall (excluding flower)
Shown on page 26.

SHOPPING LIST

Yarn (Medium Weight) 4

- ☐ Peach - 70 yards (64 meters)
- ☐ Green - 70 yards (64 meters)
- ☐ White - 36 yards (33 meters)
- ☐ Sage - 35 yards (32 meters)
- ☐ Dark Brown - 25 yards (23 meters)
- ☐ Brown - 25 yards (23 meters)
- ☐ Pink - 25 yards (23 meters)
- ☐ Dark Pink - 12 yards (11 meters)
- ☐ Gold - small amount
- ☐ Black - small amount

Crochet Hook

- ☐ Size G (4 mm)

Additional Supplies

- ☐ Yarn needle
- ☐ Polyester fiberfill
- ☐ 10.5 mm Blue safety eyes - 2 (Please take caution if the toy is for a child that is at risk of choking. See Safety, page 45.)

GAUGE INFORMATION

Gauge is **not** of great importance as long as your crochet fabric is very dense *(see Gauge, page 44)*.

—— STITCH GUIDE ——

TREBLE CROCHET *(abbreviated tr)*
YO twice, insert hook in st indicated, YO and pull up a loop (4 loops on hook), (YO and draw through 2 loops on hook) 3 times.

SINGLE CROCHET 2 TOGETHER *(abbreviated sc2tog)*
Pull up a loop in each of next 2 sc, YO and draw through all 3 loops on hook (counts as one sc).

Head

Rnd 1 (Right side)**:** With Peach, make an adjustable loop to form a ring *(Figs. 1a-d, page 45)*; work 6 sc in ring; do **not** join, place marker to indicate beginning of rnd *(see Markers, page 45)*.

Rnd 2: 2 Sc in each sc around: 12 sc.

Rnd 3: (Sc in next sc, 2 sc in next sc) around: 18 sc.

Rnd 4: (Sc in next 2 sc, 2 sc in next sc) around: 24 sc.

Rnd 5: (Sc in next 3 sc, 2 sc in next sc) around: 30 sc.

Rnds 6-11: Sc in each sc around.

Rnd 12: (Sc2tog, sc in next 3 sc) around: 24 sc.

Rnd 13: (Sc2tog, sc in next 2 sc) around: 18 sc.

Attach safety eyes to Head, placing them on Rnd 7 and spacing them approximately 4 sc apart.

Stuff Head with polyester fiberfill.

Rnd 14: (Sc2tog, sc in next sc) around: 12 sc.

Rnd 15: Sc2tog around: 6 sc.

Continue to sc2tog around until hole is closed; slip st in next sc, finish off.

Cheek (Make 2)

Rnd 1 (Right side)**:** With Peach, make an adjustable loop to form a ring; work 6 sc in ring; do **not** join, place marker.

Rnd 2: (Sc in next sc, 2 sc in next sc) around; slip st in next sc, finish off leaving a long end for sewing: 9 sc.

Nose

Rnd 1 (Right side)**:** With Peach, make an adjustable loop to form a ring; work 6 sc in ring; do **not** join, place marker.

Rnd 2: Sc in each sc around; slip st in next sc, finish off leaving a long end for sewing.

Right Ear

Row 1: With Peach, ch 2, 4 sc in second ch from hook.

Row 2 (Right side)**:** Ch 1, turn; (sc, dc) in first sc, ch 2 tightly, dc in next sc, sc around posts of 2 dc just made, sc in same sc as last dc made, 2 sc in each of last 2 sc; finish off leaving a long end for sewing.

Left Ear

Row 1: With Peach, ch 2, 4 sc in second ch from hook.

Row 2 (Right side)**:** Ch 1, turn; 2 sc in each of first 2 sc, (sc, dc) in next sc, ch 2 tightly, dc in last sc, sc around posts of 2 dc just made, sc in same sc as last dc made; finish off leaving a long end for sewing.

Face

Eyelid (Make 2)**:** With Peach, ch 3; finish off leaving a long end for sewing.

Sew Eyelids to Head above the safety eyes.

Use whipstitch *(Figs. 5a & b, page 46)* for the method of sewing to join the pieces together.

Use photos as guides for placement of all pieces. See Tips, page 45.

Sew Nose to Rnds 9-11 of Head. Sew Cheeks on each side of Nose, just below eyes, lightly stuffing with polyester fiberfill.

Pinch the area between the eyes together to form a bridge and make a couple of stitches from side to side near the inner eyes to hold it in place.

Sew Ears to Head.

With Dark Pink, embroider mouth using backstitch *(Fig. 6, page 46)*. With Black, embroider 2 eyelashes for each eye using straight stitch *(Fig. 7, page 46)*.

With Dark Brown, embroider eyebrows using straight stitch.

Body

Rnd 1 (Right side)**:** With Green, make an adjustable loop to form a ring; work 6 sc in ring; do **not** join, place marker.

Rnd 2: 2 Sc in each sc around: 12 sc.

Rnd 3: (Sc in next sc, 2 sc in next sc) around: 18 sc.

Rnd 4: (Sc in next 2 sc, 2 sc in next sc) around: 24 sc.

Rnd 5: (Sc in next 3 sc, 2 sc in next sc) around: 30 sc.

Rnd 6: Sc in each sc around.

Rnd 7: Sc in each sc around changing to Brown in last sc *(Fig. 4a, page 46)*; cut Green.

Rnds 8-11: Sc in each sc around.

Rnd 12: (Sc2tog, sc in next 3 sc) around: 24 sc.

Rnds 13 and 14: Sc in each sc around.

Rnd 15: (Sc2tog, sc in next 2 sc) around changing to Peach in last sc; cut Brown: 18 sc.

Rnd 16: Sc in Back Loop Only of each sc around *(Fig. 2, page 45)*.

Rnd 17: Sc in both loops of each sc around; slip st in next sc, finish off leaving a long end for sewing.

Stuff Body with polyester fiberfill and sew to Head.

SKIRT LEAF
Make 10 each of Green and 10 each of Sage.

Ch 5.

Rnd 1 (Right side)**:** Dc in second ch from hook, hdc in next ch, sc in next ch, (slip st, ch 2 tightly, slip st) in last ch; working in free loops of beginning ch *(Fig. 3b, page 46)*, sc in next ch, hdc in next ch, (dc, sc) in next ch, slip st around post of first dc; finish off leaving a long end for sewing.

Sew Green Leaves to every third st on Rnd 6 of Body. Sew Sage Leaves to Rnd 7 of Body between Green Leaves.

Leg (Make 2)
UPPER LEG

Rnd 1 (Right side)**:** With Green, make an adjustable loop to form a ring; work 6 sc in ring; do **not** join, place marker.

Rnd 2: (Sc in next sc, 2 sc in next sc) around: 9 sc.

Rnd 3: Sc in each sc around; slip st in next sc, finish off leaving a long end for sewing.

SHOE

With Sage, work same as Upper Leg.

LOWER LEG

Rnd 1 (Right side)**:** With Sage, make an adjustable loop to form a ring; work 6 sc in ring; do **not** join, place marker.

Rnd 2: (Sc in next sc, 2 sc in next sc) around: 9 sc.

Rnd 3: Sc in each sc around.

Rnd 4: Sc in each sc around changing to Peach in last sc; cut Sage.

Rnd 5: Sc in Back Loop Only of each sc around.

Rnds 6-10: Sc in both loops of each sc around.

Slip st in next sc, finish off leaving a long end for sewing.

Stuff all Leg pieces firmly with polyester fiberfill.

Sew Upper Legs to Body. Sew Lower Legs to Upper Legs, adding additional stuffing until they are stiff enough to hold up the body weight. Sew Shoes to front of Lower Legs.

With Peach, embroider a star on top of Shoe using 3 straight stitches.

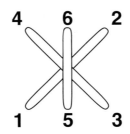

Arm (Make 2)

Rnd 1 (Right side)**:** With Peach, make an adjustable loop to form a ring; work 6 sc in ring; do **not** join, place marker.

Rnd 2: (Sc in next sc, 2 sc in next sc) around: 9 sc.

Rnds 3-9: Sc in each sc around.

Slip st in next sc, finish off leaving a long end for sewing.

Shoulder (Make 2)

Work same as Arm through Rnd 2: 9 sc.

Rnd 3: Sc in each sc around changing to Brown in last sc; cut Peach.

Rnd 4: Sc in each sc around; slip st in next sc, finish off leaving a long end for sewing.

Hand (Make 2)
FINGER (Make 4)

Rnd 1 (Right side)**:** With Peach, make an adjustable loop to form a ring; working tightly, work 5 sc in ring; do **not** join, place marker.

Rnds 2 and 3: Sc in each sc around.

Finish off first 3 Fingers only.

PALM & BACK

Rnd 1 (Joining rnd)**:** Sc in next 3 sc, sc in any sc on next 2 Fingers, sc in 3 sc on last Finger; sc in sc on opposite side of next 2 middle Fingers, place marker: 10 sc.

Rnds 2 and 3: Sc in each sc around.

Slip st in next sc, finish off leaving a long end for sewing.

Stuff Shoulders, Arms, and Hands with polyester fiberfill.

Sew Shoulders to Body.
Sew Arms to Shoulders, positioning them as shown.

Sew Hands to beginning end of Arms; sew spaces between Fingers closed.

Hair

Cut approximately 75 strands of Dark Brown, each 10" (25.5 cm) long.

Fold one strand in half. Using a crochet hook, draw the folded end up through a stitch on the Head and pull the loose ends through the folded end *(Fig. A)*; draw the knot up tightly. Repeat, spacing strands to cover Head.

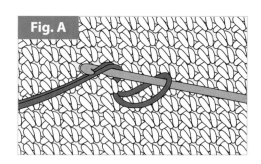

Fig. A

Large Wing (Make 2)

With Pink, ch 12.

Rnd 1 (Right side)**:** Dc in third ch from hook and in next 8 chs, 6 dc in last ch; working in free loops of beginning ch, dc in next 8 chs, 4 dc in next ch; skip beginning ch and join with slip st to first dc: 27 dc.

Note: Loop a short piece of yarn around any stitch to mark Rnd 1 as **right** side.

Begin working in rows.

Row 1: Slip st in next 2 dc, sc in next 4 dc, hdc in next 3 dc, 2 dc in each of next 4 dc, hdc in next 3 dc, sc in next 4 dc, slip st in next 3 dc, leave remaining dc unworked; finish off leaving a long end for sewing.

Row 2: With **right** side facing, join Sage with slip st in first sc; slip st in next 2 sc, sc in next 3 sts, hdc in next hdc, 2 hdc in each of next 2 dc, (hdc, dc) in next dc, 2 dc in next dc, ch 1, 2 dc in next dc, (dc, hdc) in next dc, 2 hdc in each of next 2 dc, hdc in next hdc, sc in next 3 sts, slip st in next 3 sc, leave remaining slip sts unworked; finish off.

29

Row 3: With **right** side facing, join Dark Pink with slip st in first sc; slip st in next 2 sc, sc in next 6 hdc, (sc, hdc) in next dc, (hdc, dc) in next dc, (dc, tr) in next dc, ch 1, skip next ch, (tr, dc) in next dc, (dc, hdc) in next dc, (hdc, sc) in next dc, sc in next 6 hdc, slip st in next 3 sc, leave remaining sts unworked; finish off.

Small Wing (Make 2)

With Pink, ch 6.

Rnd 1 (Right side)**:** Dc in third ch from hook and in next 2 chs, 6 dc in last ch; working in free loops of beginning ch, dc in next 2 chs, 3 dc in next ch; skip beginning ch and join with slip st to first dc: 14 dc.

Note: Mark Rnd 1 as **right** side.

Begin working in rows.

Row 1: Slip st in next dc, sc in next 3 dc, (sc, hdc) in next dc, (hdc, dc) in next dc, (dc, hdc) in next dc, (hdc, sc) in next dc, sc in next 3 dc, slip st in next dc, leave remaining dc unworked; finish off.

Row 2: With **right** side facing, join Sage with slip st in first sc; slip st in next sc, sc in next 3 sts, (sc, hdc) in next hdc, (hdc, dc) in next dc, (dc, hdc) in next dc, (hdc, sc) in next hdc, sc in next 3 sts, slip st in next 2 sc, leave remaining sts unworked; finish off.

Row 3: With **right** side facing, join Dark Pink with slip st in first sc; slip st in next sc, sc in next 3 sts, (sc, hdc) in next hdc, (hdc, dc) in next dc, (dc, hdc) in next dc, (hdc, sc) in next hdc, sc in next 3 sts, slip st in next 2 sc, leave remaining sts unworked; finish off.

Sew end of Large Wings to back of Body, spacing them 3 sc apart. Sew end of Small Wings at an angle on top of Large Wings.

Flower

PETAL (Make 6)

With White, ch 9.

Rnd 1 (Right side)**:** Dc in third ch from hook and in next 5 chs, 6 dc in last ch; working in free loops of beginning ch, dc in next 5 chs, 4 dc in next ch; skip beginning ch and join with slip st to first dc: 21 dc.

Note: Mark Rnd 1 as **right** side.

Rnd 2: Slip st in next dc, sc in next 2 dc, hdc in next 2 dc, 2 dc in each of next 6 dc, hdc in next 2 dc, sc in next 2 dc, slip st in next 2 dc, leave remaining sts unworked; finish off leaving a long end for sewing.

Fold beginning end of each Petal and sew together to form center. Sew across 2 sts on sides of Petals.

CENTER

Rnd 1 (Right side)**:** With Gold, make an adjustable loop to form a ring; work 6 sc in ring; do **not** join, place marker.

Rnd 2: 2 Sc in each sc around: 12 sc.

Rnds 3 and 4: Sc in each sc around.

Slip st in next sc, finish off leaving a long end for sewing.

Stuff Center with polyester fiberfill and sew to **right** side of Petals.

CENTER BACK

Rnd 1 (Right side)**:** With Green, make an adjustable loop to form a ring; work 6 sc in ring; do **not** join, place marker.

Rnd 2: 2 Sc in each sc around: 12 sc.

Rnd 3: Sc in each sc around; slip st in next sc, finish off leaving a long end for sewing.

Stuff Center Back with polyester fiberfill and sew behind Petals.

STEM
Rnd 1 (Right side)**:** With Green, make an adjustable loop to form a ring; work 6 sc in ring; do **not** join, place marker.

Rnd 2: (Sc in next sc, 2 sc in next sc) around: 9 sc.

Stuff Stem firmly with polyester fiberfill as you work.

Rnds 3-42: Sc in each sc around.

Slip st in next sc, finish off.

Sew Stem to the side of Center Back.

LEAF
With Green, ch 6.

Rnd 1 (Right side)**:** Dc in third ch from hook and in next 2 chs, 6 dc in last ch; working in free loops of beginning ch, dc in next 2 chs, 3 dc in next ch; skip beginning ch and join with slip st to first dc: 14 dc.

Rnd 2: Sc in next 3 dc, (sc, hdc) in next dc, (hdc, dc) in next dc, (dc, hdc) in next dc, (hdc, sc) in next dc, sc in next 3 dc, slip st in last 3 dc: 18 sts.

Rnd 3: Slip st in joining slip st and in next 2 sc, sc in next 3 sts, (sc, hdc) in next hdc, (hdc, dc) in next dc, (dc, hdc) in next dc, (hdc, sc) in next hdc, sc in next 3 sts, slip st in next 2 sc, leave remaining sts unworked; finish off leaving a long end for sewing.

Sew Leaf to Stem.

Position the Fairy so she is standing and place her left hand on the Stem to see where it will balance. Sew Stem to Hand with the top finger toward the front to look like a thumb.

31

Gnome

EASY +

Finished Size: Approximately 9" (23 cm) tall

SHOPPING LIST

Yarn (Medium Weight)

- ☐ Peach - 30 yards (27.5 meters)
- ☐ Gold - 55 yards (50.5 meters)
- ☐ Red - 30 yards (27.5 meters)
- ☐ Dark Brown - 28 yards (25.5 meters)
- ☐ Brown - 28 yards (25.5 meters)
- ☐ Light Brown - 20 yards (18.5 meters)
- ☐ Dark Pink - small amount
- ☐ Black - small amount

(Bulky Weight)

[1.76 ounces, 63 yards
(50 grams, 57 meters) per skein]:

- ☐ White bulky - 1 skein

Crochet Hook

- ☐ Size G (4 mm)

Additional Supplies

- ☐ Yarn needle
- ☐ Polyester fiberfill
- ☐ 12 mm Brown safety eyes - 2
  (Please take caution if the
  toy is for a child that is at
  risk of choking. See Safety,
  page 45.)
- ☐ White embroidery floss

GAUGE INFORMATION

Gauge is **not** of great importance as long as your crochet fabric is very dense *(see Gauge, page 44)*.

—— STITCH GUIDE ——

SINGLE CROCHET 2 TOGETHER
(abbreviated sc2tog)

Pull up a loop in each of next 2 sc, YO and draw through all 3 loops on hook **(counts as one sc)**.

Head

Rnd 1 (Right side)**:** With Peach, make an adjustable loop to form a ring *(Figs. 1a-d, page 45)*; work 6 sc in ring; do **not** join, place marker to indicate beginning of rnd *(see Markers, page 45)*.

Rnd 2: 2 Sc in each sc around: 12 sc.

Rnd 3: (Sc in next sc, 2 sc in next sc) around: 18 sc.

Rnd 4: (Sc in next 2 sc, 2 sc in next sc) around: 24 sc.

Rnd 5: (Sc in next 3 sc, 2 sc in next sc) around: 30 sc.

Rnd 6: (Sc in next 4 sc, 2 sc in next sc) around: 36 sc.

Rnd 7: Sc in each sc around changing to White bulky yarn in last sc *(Fig. 4a, page 46)*; cut Peach.

Rnds 8 and 9: Sc in each sc around.

Rnd 10: Sc in next 9 sc, sc in Front Loop Only of next 18 sc *(Fig. 2, page 45)*, sc in **both** loops of last 9 sc.

Rnd 11: Sc in next 9 sc, sc in Back Loop Only of next 18 sc, sc in **both** loops of last 9 sc.

Rnd 12: (Sc2tog, sc in next 4 sc) around: 30 sc.

Rnd 13: (Sc2tog, sc in next 3 sc) around: 24 sc.

Rnd 14: (Sc2tog, sc in next 2 sc) around: 18 sc.

Attach safety eyes to Head, placing them on Rnd 4 and spacing them approximately 6 sc apart.

Stuff Head with polyester fiberfill.

Rnd 15: (Sc2tog, sc in next sc) around: 12 sc.

Rnd 16: Sc2tog around: 6 sc.

Continue to sc2tog around until hole is closed; slip st in next sc, finish off.

Cheek (Make 2)

Rnd 1 (Right side)**:** With Peach, make an adjustable loop to form a ring; work 6 sc in ring; do **not** join, place marker.

Rnd 2: 2 Sc in each sc around: 12 sc.

Rnd 3: Sc in each sc around; slip st in next sc, finish off leaving a long end for sewing.

Nose

Rnd 1 (Right side)**:** With Peach, make an adjustable loop to form a ring; work 6 sc in ring; do **not** join, place marker.

Rnd 2: Sc in each sc around; slip st in next sc, finish off leaving a long end for sewing.

Face

Eyelid (Make 2): With Peach, ch 3; finish off leaving a long end for sewing.

Sew Eyelids to Head above the safety eyes.

Use whipstitch *(Figs. 5a & b, page 46)* for the method of sewing to join the pieces together.

Use photos as guides for placement of all pieces. See Tips, page 45.

Sew Nose to Rnds 1 and 2 of Head. Sew Cheeks on each side of Nose, just below eyes, stuffing with polyester fiberfill.

Pinch the area between the eyes together to form a bridge and make a couple of stitches from side to side near the inner eyes to hold it in place.

With Dark Pink, embroider mouth using backstitch *(Fig. 6, page 46)*.

Hat

Rnd 1 (Right side): With Red, make an adjustable loop to form a ring; work 6 sc in ring; do **not** join, place marker.

Rnds 2 and 3: Sc in each sc around.

Rnd 4: 2 Sc in each sc around: 12 sc.

Rnds 5 and 6: Sc in each sc around.

Rnd 7: (Sc in next sc, 2 sc in next sc) around: 18 sc.

Rnds 8 and 9: Sc in each sc around.

Rnd 10: (Sc in next 2 sc, 2 sc in next sc) around: 24 sc.

Rnds 11 and 12: Sc in each sc around.

Rnd 13: (Sc in next 3 sc, 2 sc in next sc) around: 30 sc.

Rnds 14 and 15: Sc in each sc around.

Rnd 16: (Sc in next 4 sc, 2 sc in next sc) around: 36 sc.

Rnds 17 and 18: Sc in each sc around.

Slip st in next sc, finish off leaving a long end for sewing.

Stuff Hat with polyester fiberfill and sew Back Loops Only of last rnd to top of Head.

Body

Rnd 1 (Right side): With Brown, make an adjustable loop to form a ring; work 6 sc in ring; do **not** join, place marker.

Rnd 2: 2 Sc in each sc around: 12 sc.

Rnd 3: (Sc in next sc, 2 sc in next sc) around: 18 sc.

Rnd 4: (Sc in next 2 sc, 2 sc in next sc) around: 24 sc.

Rnd 5: (Sc in next 3 sc, 2 sc in next sc) around: 30 sc.

Rnd 6: (Sc in next 4 sc, 2 sc in next sc) around: 36 sc.

Rnd 7: (Sc in next 5 sc, 2 sc in next sc) around: 42 sc.

Rnd 8: (Sc in next 6 sc, 2 sc in next sc) around: 48 sc.

Rnds 9 and 10: Sc in each sc around.

Rnd 11: Sc in each sc around changing to Gold in last sc; cut Brown.

Rnd 12: Sc in Back Loop Only of each sc around.

Rnds 13-16: Sc in both loops of each sc around.

Rnd 17: (Sc2tog, sc in next 6 sc) around: 42 sc.

Rnd 18: Sc in each sc around.

Rnd 19: (Sc2tog, sc in next 5 sc) around: 36 sc.

Rnd 20: (Sc2tog, sc in next 4 sc) around: 30 sc.

Rnd 21: (Sc2tog, sc in next 3 sc) around; slip st in next sc, finish off leaving a long end for sewing: 24 sc.

Stuff Body with polyester fiberfill and sew to the Head.

Arm (Make 2)

Rnd 1 (Right side)**:** With Gold, make an adjustable loop to form a ring; work 6 sc in ring; do **not** join, place marker.

Rnd 2: 2 Sc in each sc around: 12 sc.

Rnds 3-7: Sc in each sc around.

Slip st in next sc, finish off leaving a long end for sewing.

Shoulder (Make 2)

Work same as Arm through Rnd 5.

Slip st in next sc, finish off leaving a long end for sewing.

Hand (Make 2)
FINGER (Make 4)

Rnd 1 (Right side)**:** With Peach, make an adjustable loop to form a ring; working tightly, work 5 sc in ring; do **not** join, place marker.

Rnds 2 and 3: Sc in each sc around.

Finish off first 3 Fingers only.

PALM & BACK

Rnd 1 (Joining rnd)**:** Sc in next 3 sc, sc in any sc on next 2 Fingers, sc in 3 sc on last Finger; sc in sc on opposite side of next 2 middle Fingers, place marker: 10 sc.

Rnds 2 and 3: Sc in each sc around.

Slip st in next sc, finish off leaving a long end for sewing.

Stuff Shoulders, Arms, and Hands with polyester fiberfill.

Sew Shoulders to Body.
Sew Arms to Shoulders, positioning them as shown.

Sew Hands to beginning end of Arms; sew spaces between Fingers closed.

Suspender (Make 2): With Brown, ch 30; finish off leaving a long end for sewing.

Sew each end of both Suspenders to Rnd 11 of Body, crossing them in the back.

Tack left Hand to belly.

Shoe (Make 2)

Rnd 1 (Right side): With Dark Brown, make an adjustable loop to form a ring; work 6 sc in ring; do **not** join, place marker.

Rnd 2: 2 Sc in each sc around: 12 sc.

Rnd 3: (Sc in next sc, 2 sc in next sc) around: 18 sc.

Rnd 4: (Sc in next 2 sc, 2 sc in next sc) around: 24 sc.

Rnd 5: Sc in Back Loop Only of next 9 sc, working in **both** loops, (2 sc in next sc, sc in next sc) 3 times, sc in Back Loop Only of next 9 sc: 27 sc.

Rnds 6 and 7: Sc in both loops of each sc around.

Rnd 8: Sc in next 9 sc, sc2tog 4 times, sc in next 10 sc: 23 sc.

Rnd 9: Sc in next 5 sc, sc2tog 6 times, sc in next 6 sc changing to Brown in last sc; cut Dark Brown: 17 sc.

Rnd 10: Sc in each sc around; slip st in next sc, finish off leaving a long end for sewing.

Stuff Shoes with polyester fiberfill.

Sew Shoes to Body placing shaping towards the Front.

Walking Staff

STICK

Rnd 1 (Right side): With Light Brown and leaving a long end for sewing, make an adjustable loop to form a ring; work 6 sc in ring; do **not** join, place marker.

Rnd 2: 2 Sc in each sc around: 12 sc.

Rnd 3: Sc in Back Loop Only of each sc around.

Rnds 4-11: Sc in both loops of each sc around.

Rnd 12: (Sc2tog, sc in next sc) around: 8 sc.

Stuff Stick firmly with polyester fiberfill as you work.

Rnds 13-20: Sc in each sc around.

Rnd 21: Sc2tog around: 6 sc.

Continue to sc2tog around until hole is closed; slip st in next sc, finish off.

BRANCH
Rnd 1 (Right side)**:** With Light Brown, make an adjustable loop to form a ring; work 6 sc in ring; do **not** join, place marker.

Rnd 2: (Sc in next 2 sc, 2 sc in next sc) twice: 8 sc.

Rnd 3: Sc in Back Loop Only of each sc around.

Rnds 4 and 5: Sc in both loops of each sc around.

Rnd 6: (Sc in next 2 sc, sc2tog) twice: 6 sc.

Rnd 7: Sc in each sc around; slip st in next sc, finish off leaving a long end for sewing.

Stuff Branch with polyester fiberfill and sew to Stick.

LADY BUG
Rnd 1 (Right side)**:** With Red, make an adjustable loop to form a ring; work 6 sc in ring; join with slip st to first sc, finish off leaving a long end for sewing.

With Black, embroider line across Lady Bug using backstitch. Embroider head using satin stitch *(Fig. 8a, page 47)*. Make 3 dots on each side of center line using French knots *(Fig. 9, page 47)*.

With White embroidery floss, embroider eyes using small straight stitches *(Fig. 7, page 46)*.

Sew Lady Bug to Stick.

Position the Gnome so he is standing and place his right hand on the Stick to see where it will balance.
Sew Stick in place.

Gnomette

EASY +

Finished Size: Approximately 9" (23 cm) tall (excluding flower)

SHOPPING LIST

Yarn (Medium Weight) [MEDIUM 4]

- ☐ Peach - 30 yards (27.5 meters)
- ☐ Yellow - 58 yards (53 meters)
- ☐ White - 52 yards (47.5 meters)
- ☐ Red - 35 yards (32 meters)
- ☐ Brown - 34 yards (31 meters)
- ☐ Dark Brown - 32 yards (29.5 meters)
- ☐ Gold - 32 yards (29.5 meters)
- ☐ Green - 32 yards (29.5 meters)
- ☐ Dark Pink - small amount
- ☐ Black - small amount

Crochet Hook

- ☐ Size G (4 mm)

Additional Supplies

- ☐ Yarn needle
- ☐ Polyester fiberfill
- ☐ 12 mm Brown safety eyes - 2 (Please take caution if the toy is for a child that is at risk of choking. See Safety, page 45.)

GAUGE INFORMATION

Gauge is **not** of great importance as long as your crochet fabric is very dense *(see Gauge, page 44)*.

—— STITCH GUIDE ——

SINGLE CROCHET 2 TOGETHER
(abbreviated sc2tog)

Pull up a loop in each of next 2 sc, YO and draw through all 3 loops on hook (**counts as one sc**).

Head

Rnd 1 (Right side)**:** With Peach, make an adjustable loop to form a ring *(Figs. 1a-d, page 45)*; work 6 sc in ring; do **not** join, place marker to indicate beginning of rnd *(see Markers, page 45)*.

Rnd 2: 2 Sc in each sc around: 12 sc.

Rnd 3: (Sc in next sc, 2 sc in next sc) around: 18 sc.

Rnd 4: (Sc in next 2 sc, 2 sc in next sc) around: 24 sc.

Rnd 5: (Sc in next 3 sc, 2 sc in next sc) around: 30 sc.

Rnd 6: (Sc in next 4 sc, 2 sc in next sc) around: 36 sc.

Rnds 7-11: Sc in each sc around.

Rnd 12: (Sc2tog, sc in next 4 sc) around: 30 sc.

Rnd 13: (Sc2tog, sc in next 3 sc) around: 24 sc.

Rnd 14: (Sc2tog, sc in next 2 sc) around: 18 sc.

Attach safety eyes to Head, placing them on Rnd 7 and spacing them approximately 6 sc apart.

Stuff Head with polyester fiberfill.

Rnd 15: (Sc2tog, sc in next sc) around: 12 sc.

Rnd 16: Sc2tog around: 6 sc.

Continue to sc2tog around until hole is closed; slip st in next sc, finish off.

Cheek (Make 2)

Rnd 1 (Right side)**:** With Peach, make an adjustable loop to form a ring; work 6 sc in ring; do **not** join, place marker.

Rnd 2: 2 Sc in each sc around: 12 sc.

Rnd 3: Sc in each sc around; slip st in next sc, finish off leaving a long end for sewing.

Nose

Rnd 1 (Right side)**:** With Peach, make an adjustable loop to form a ring; work 6 sc in ring; do **not** join, place marker.

Rnd 2: Sc in each sc around; slip st in next sc, finish off leaving a long end for sewing.

Face

Eyelid (Make 2)**:** With Peach, ch 3; finish off leaving a long end for sewing.

Sew Eyelids to Head above the safety eyes.

Use whipstitch *(Figs. 5a & b, page 46)* for the method of sewing to join the pieces together.

Use photos as guides for placement of all pieces. See Tips, page 45.

Sew Nose to Rnds 9-11 of Head. Sew Cheeks on each side of Nose, just below eyes, stuffing with polyester fiberfill.

Pinch the area between the eyes together to form a bridge and make a couple of stitches from side to side near the inner eyes to hold it in place.

With Dark Pink, embroider mouth using backstitch *(Fig. 6, page 46)*. With Black, embroider 2 eyelashes for each eye using straight stitch *(Fig. 7, page 46)*.

Hat

Rnd 1 (Right side)**:** With Red, make an adjustable loop to form a ring; work 6 sc in ring; do **not** join, place marker.

Rnds 2 and 3: Sc in each sc around.

Rnd 4: 2 Sc in each sc around: 12 sc.

Rnds 5 and 6: Sc in each sc around.

Rnd 7: (Sc in next sc, 2 sc in next sc) around: 18 sc.

Rnds 8 and 9: Sc in each sc around.

Rnd 10: (Sc in next 2 sc, 2 sc in next sc) around: 24 sc.

Rnds 11 and 12: Sc in each sc around.

Rnd 13: (Sc in next 3 sc, 2 sc in next sc) around: 30 sc.

Rnds 14 and 15: Sc in each sc around.

Rnd 16: (Sc in next 4 sc, 2 sc in next sc) around: 36 sc.

Rnds 17 and 18: Sc in each sc around.

Slip st in next sc, finish off leaving a long end for sewing.

Bow (Make 2)
With Red, ch 6.

Rnd 1: Dc in third ch from hook and in next 2 chs, 6 dc in last ch; working in free loops of beginning ch *(Fig. 3b, page 46)*, dc in next 2 chs, 4 dc in next ch; join with slip st to top of beginning ch, finish off leaving a long end for sewing.

Tightly wrap the yarn end around center; secure, do **not** cut yarn.

Hair

Cut approximately 25 strands of White, each 12" (30.5 cm) long, for each braid.

Place Hat on Head as a guide for placement of Hair.

Fold one strand in half. Using a crochet hook, draw the folded end up through a stitch on the Head and pull the loose ends through the folded end *(Fig. A, page 29)*; draw the knot up tightly.
Repeat spacing strands to form hair line.

Braid yarn on one side of Head, then wrap yarn from Bow around bottom of braid; make a knot in back of Bow. Repeat for second side.

Stuff Hat with polyester fiberfill and sew Back Loops Only of last rnd to top of Head.

Body

Rnd 1 (Right side)**:** With Brown, make an adjustable loop to form a ring; work 6 sc in ring; do **not** join, place marker.

Rnd 2: 2 Sc in each sc around: 12 sc.

Rnd 3: (Sc in next sc, 2 sc in next sc) around: 18 sc.

Rnd 4: (Sc in next 2 sc, 2 sc in next sc) around: 24 sc.

Rnd 5: (Sc in next 3 sc, 2 sc in next sc) around: 30 sc.

Rnd 6: (Sc in next 4 sc, 2 sc in next sc) around: 36 sc.

Rnd 7: (Sc in next 5 sc, 2 sc in next sc) around: 42 sc.

Rnd 8: (Sc in next 6 sc, 2 sc in next sc) around: 48 sc.

Rnds 9 and 10: Sc in each sc around.

Rnd 11: Sc in each sc around changing to Yellow in last sc; cut Brown.

Rnd 12: Sc in Back Loop Only of each sc around *(Fig. 2, page 45)*.

Rnds 13-16: Sc in both loops of each sc around.

Rnd 17: (Sc2tog, sc in next 6 sc) around: 42 sc.

Rnd 18: Sc in each sc around.

Rnd 19: (Sc2tog, sc in next 5 sc) around: 36 sc.

Rnd 20: (Sc2tog, sc in next 4 sc) around: 30 sc.

Rnd 21: (Sc2tog, sc in next 3 sc) around; slip st in next sc, finish off leaving a long end for sewing: 24 sc.

SKIRT

Rnd 1 (Wrong side)**:** With beginning end toward you and working in free loops of Rnd 11 on Body *(Fig. 3a, page 46)*, join Gold with slip st in first sc; ch 3 **(counts as first dc, now and throughout)**, dc in next sc and in each sc around; join with slip st to first dc: 48 dc.

Rnds 2-4: Ch 3, dc in next dc and in each dc around; join with slip st to first dc.

Finish off.

Rnd 5: Turn Skirt down. With **right** side facing, join Brown with slip st in same st as joining; ch 3, dc in next dc and in each dc around; join with slip st to first dc, finish off.

Stuff Body with polyester fiberfill and sew to Head.

Arm (Make 2)

Rnd 1 (Right side)**:** With Yellow, make an adjustable loop to form a ring; work 6 sc in ring; do **not** join, place marker.

Rnd 2: 2 Sc in each sc around: 12 sc.

Rnds 3-7: Sc in each sc around.

Slip st in next sc, finish off leaving a long end for sewing.

Shoulder (Make 2)

Work same as Arm through Rnd 5: 12 sc.

Slip st in next sc, finish off leaving a long end for sewing.

Hand (Make 2)

FINGER (Make 4)

Rnd 1 (Right side): With Peach, make an adjustable loop to form a ring; working tightly, work 5 sc in ring; do **not** join, place marker.

Rnds 2 and 3: Sc in each sc around.

Finish off first 3 Fingers only.

PALM & BACK

Rnd 1 (Joining rnd): Sc in next 3 sc, sc in any sc on next 2 Fingers, sc in 3 sc on last Finger; sc in sc on opposite side of next 2 middle Fingers, place marker: 10 sc.

Rnds 2 and 3: Sc in each sc around.

Slip st in next sc, finish off leaving a long end for sewing.

Stuff Shoulders, Arms, and Hands with polyester fiberfill.

Sew Shoulders to Body.
Sew Arms to Shoulders, positioning them as shown.

Sew Hands to beginning end of Arms; sew spaces between Fingers closed.

Shoe (Make 2)

Rnd 1 (Right side): With Dark Brown, make an adjustable loop to form a ring; work 6 sc in ring; do **not** join, place marker.

Rnd 2: 2 Sc in each sc around: 12 sc.

Rnd 3: (Sc in next sc, 2 sc in next sc) around: 18 sc.

Rnd 4: (Sc in next 2 sc, 2 sc in next sc) around: 24 sc.

Rnd 5: Sc in Back Loop Only of next 9 sc, working in **both** loops, (2 sc in next sc, sc in next sc) 3 times, sc in Back Loop Only of next 9 sc: 27 sc.

Rnds 6 and 7: Sc in both loops of each sc around.

Rnd 8: Sc in next 9 sc, sc2tog 4 times, sc in next 10 sc: 23 sc.

Rnd 9: Sc in next 5 sc, sc2tog 6 times, sc in next 6 sc; slip st in next sc, finish off leaving a long end for sewing: 17 sc.

Stuff Shoes with polyester fiberfill.

Sew Shoes to Body placing shaping towards the Front.

Flower

PETAL (Make 6)
With White, ch 9.

Rnd 1 (Right side)**:** Dc in third ch from hook and in next 5 chs, 6 dc in last ch; working in free loops of beginning ch, dc in next 5 chs, 4 dc in next ch; skip beginning ch and join with slip st to first dc: 21 dc.

Note: Loop a short piece of yarn around any stitch to mark Rnd 1 as **right** side.

Rnd 2: Slip st in next dc, sc in next 2 dc, hdc in next 2 dc, 2 dc in each of next 6 dc, hdc in next 2 dc, sc in next 2 dc, slip st in next 2 dc, leave remaining sts unworked; finish off leaving a long end for sewing.

Fold beginning end of each Petal and sew together to form center. Sew across 7 sts on sides of Petals.

CENTER
Rnd 1 (Right side)**:** With Yellow, make an adjustable loop to form a ring; work 6 sc in ring; do **not** join, place marker.

Rnd 2: 2 Sc in each sc around: 12 sc.

Rnds 3 and 4: Sc in each sc around.

Slip st in next sc, finish off leaving a long end for sewing.

Stuff Center with polyester fiberfill and sew to **right** side of Petals.

CENTER BACK
Rnd 1 (Right side)**:** With Green, make an adjustable loop to form a ring; work 6 sc in ring; do **not** join, place marker.

Rnd 2: 2 Sc in each sc around: 12 sc.

Rnd 3: Sc in each sc around; slip st in next sc, finish off leaving a long end for sewing.

Stuff Center Back with polyester fiberfill and sew behind Petals.

STEM
Rnd 1 (Right side)**:** With Green, make an adjustable loop to form a ring; work 6 sc in ring; do **not** join, place marker.

Rnd 2: (Sc in next sc, 2 sc in next sc) around: 9 sc.

Stuff Stem firmly with polyester fiberfill as you work.

Rnds 3-39: Sc in each sc around.

Slip st in next sc, finish off.

Sew Stem to the side of Center Back.

LEAF
With Green, ch 6.

Rnd 1 (Right side)**:** Dc in third ch from hook and in next 2 chs, 6 dc in last ch; working in free loops of beginning ch, dc in next 2 chs, 3 dc in next ch; skip beginning ch and join with slip st to first dc: 14 dc.

Rnd 2: Sc in next 3 dc, (sc, hdc) in next dc, (hdc, dc) in next dc, (dc, hdc) in next dc, (hdc, sc) in next dc, sc in next 3 dc, slip st in last 3 dc: 18 sts.

Rnd 3: Slip st in joining slip st and in next 2 sc, sc in next 3 sts, (sc, hdc) in next hdc, (hdc, dc) in next dc, (dc, hdc) in next dc, (hdc, sc) in next hdc, sc in next 3 sts, slip st in next 2 sc, leave remaining sts unworked; finish off leaving a long end for sewing.

Sew Leaf to Stem.

Position the Gnomette so she is standing and place her left hand on the Stem to see where it will balance. Sew Stem to Hand with the top finger toward the front to look like a thumb.

General Instructions

ABBREVIATIONS

ch(s)	chain(s)
cm	centimeters
dc	double crochet(s)
hdc	half double crochet(s)
mm	millimeters
Rnd(s)	Round(s)
sc	single crochet(s)
sc2tog	single crochet 2 together
sp(s)	space(s)
st(s)	stitch(es)
tr	treble crochet(s)
YO	yarn over

SYMBOLS & TERMS

★ — work instructions following ★ as many **more** times as indicated in addition to the first time.

† to † — work all instructions from first † to second † **as many** times as specified.

( ) or [ ] — work enclosed instructions **as many** times as specified by the number immediately following **or** work all enclosed instructions in the stitch or space indicated **or** contains explanatory remarks.

colon (:) — the number(s) given after a colon at the end of a row or round denote(s) the number of stitches or spaces you should have on that row or round.

GAUGE

Gauge is not of great importance; your project may be a little larger or smaller without changing the overall effect. Be sure your crochet fabric is dense enough so that stuffing does not show through your stitches. Use the size hook needed to achieve a tight gauge.

CROCHET TERMINOLOGY	
UNITED STATES	INTERNATIONAL
slip stitch (slip st)	= single crochet (sc)
single crochet (sc)	= double crochet (dc)
half double crochet (hdc)	= half treble crochet (htr)
double crochet (dc)	= treble crochet (tr)
treble crochet (tr)	= double treble crochet (dtr)
double treble crochet (dtr)	= triple treble crochet (ttr)
triple treble crochet (tr tr)	= quadruple treble crochet (qtr)
skip	= miss

Yarn Weight Symbol & Names	LACE 0	SUPER FINE 1	FINE 2	LIGHT 3	MEDIUM 4	BULKY 5	SUPER BULKY 6	JUMBO 7
Type of Yarns in Category	Fingering, size 10 crochet thread	Sock, Fingering, Baby	Sport, Baby	DK, Light Worsted	Worsted, Afghan, Aran	Chunky, Craft, Rug	Super Bulky, Roving	Jumbo, Roving
Crochet Gauge* Ranges in Single Crochet to 4" (10 cm)	32-42 sts**	21-32 sts	16-20 sts	12-17 sts	11-14 sts	8-11 sts	6-9 sts	5 sts and fewer
Advised Hook Size Range	Steel*** 6 to 8, Regular hook B-1	B-1 to E-4	E-4 to 7	7 to I-9	I-9 to K-10½	K-10½ to M/N-13	M/N-13 to Q	Q and larger

*GUIDELINES ONLY: The chart above reflects the most commonly used gauges and hook sizes for specific yarn categories.

** Lace weight yarns are usually crocheted with larger hooks to create lacy openwork patterns. Accordingly, a gauge range is difficult to determine. Always follow the gauge stated in your pattern.

*** Steel crochet hooks are sized differently from regular hooks–the higher the number, the smaller the hook, which is the reverse of regular hook sizing.

▰▱▱▱ BEGINNER	Projects for first-time crocheters using basic stitches. Minimal shaping.
▰▰▱▱ EASY	Projects using yarn with basic stitches, repetitive stitch patterns, simple color changes, and simple shaping and finishing.
▰▰▰▱ INTERMEDIATE	Projects using a variety of techniques, such as basic lace patterns or color patterns, mid-level shaping and finishing.
▰▰▰▰ EXPERIENCED	Projects with intricate stitch patterns, techniques and dimension, such as non-repeating patterns, multi-color techniques, fine threads, small hooks, detailed shaping and refined finishing.

ADJUSTABLE LOOP

Wind the yarn around two fingers to form a ring *(Fig. 1a)*, slide the yarn off your fingers and grasp the strands at the top of the ring *(Fig. 1b)*. Insert the hook from **front** to **back** into the ring, pull up a loop, YO and draw through the loop on hook to lock the ring *(Fig. 1c)*.

Working around **both** strands, work stitches in the ring as specified, then pull the yarn end to close *(Fig. 1d)*.

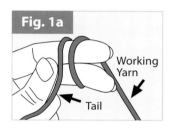

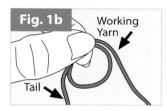

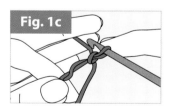

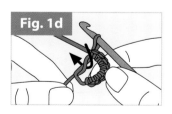

TIPS

SAFETY

If the item is for a child that is at risk of choking, do **not** use beads or buttons as a substitute for the safety eyes. When using safety eyes, it is important to make sure the eyes are attached correctly by following the directions on the package. Make sure that they can't work their way through the crocheted stitches. When in doubt, embroider the eyes instead *(see Embroidery Stitches, page 46)*.

STUFFING

Add plenty of polyester fiberfill to the crocheted pieces to maintain the shape, but not so much that it will show through your stitches. The legs of the standing animals and the fairy need to be stuffed firmly so that they are stiff enough to hold the weight of the body. Hold each leg as you are stuffing it in such a way as to prevent it from being stretched out of shape.

YARN ENDS

Instead of weaving in yarn ends, they can be inserted into the center of the stuffed parts. Make sure that the yarn used for embroidery is inserted in the center of the piece and doesn't show.

MARKERS

Markers are used to help distinguish the beginning of each round being worked. Place a 2" (5 cm) scrap piece of yarn before the first stitch of each round, moving the marker after each round is complete.

BACK OR FRONT LOOP ONLY

Work only in loop(s) indicated by arrow *(Fig. 2)*.

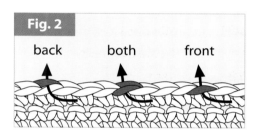

CROCHET HOOKS																
U.S.	B-1	C-2	D-3	E-4	F-5	G-6	7	H-8	I-9	J-10	K-10½	L-11	M/N-13	N/P-15	P/Q	Q	S
Metric - mm	2.25	2.75	3.25	3.5	3.75	4	4.5	5	5.5	6	6.5	8	9	10	15	16	19

FREE LOOPS

After working in Back or Front Loops Only on a row or round, there will be a ridge of unused loops. These are called the free loops. Later, when instructed to work in the free loops of the same row or round, work in these loops *(Fig. 3a)*.

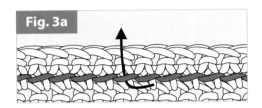
Fig. 3a

When instructed to work in free loops of a chain, work in loop indicated by arrow *(Fig. 3b)*.

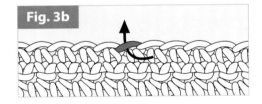
Fig. 3b

CHANGING COLORS

To change colors while working a sc, pull up a loop in stitch indicated (2 loops on hook), drop yarn, hook new yarn *(Fig. 4a)* and draw through both loops on hook. Do **not** cut yarn unless indicated.

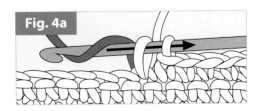
Fig. 4a

To change colors while joining with a slip st, drop yarn, insert hook in first st *(Fig. 4b)*, hook new yarn and draw through st **and** loop on hook.

Fig. 4b

WHIPSTITCH

To sew a piece to another, insert the needle from **front** to **back** through two strands of a stitch **or** end of a row on the top piece, then through a stitch on the bottom piece *(Figs. 5a & b)*. Bring the needle around and insert it through the next strands on the top piece, then through a stitch on the bottom piece. Continue working in same manner.

Fig. 5a

Fig. 5b

EMBROIDERY STITCHES
BACKSTITCH

Backstitch is worked from **right** to **left**. Come up at 1, go down at 2 and come up at 3 *(Fig. 6)*. The second stitch is made by going down at 1 and coming up at 4.

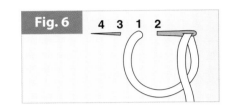
Fig. 6   4 3 1 2

STRAIGHT STITCH

Straight stitch is just what the name implies, a single, straight stitch. Come up at 1 and go down at 2 *(Fig. 7)*.

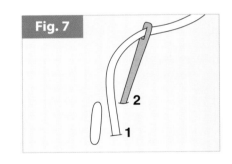
Fig. 7

SATIN STITCH

Satin stitch is a series of straight stitches worked side by side that touch but do not overlap *(Fig. 8a)* **or** come out of and go into the same stitch *(Fig. 8b)*. Come up at odd numbers and go down at even numbers.

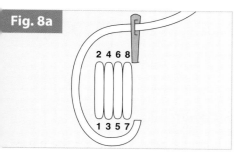

Fig. 8a

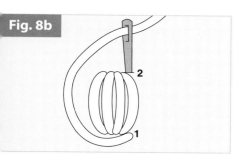

Fig. 8b

FRENCH KNOT

Bring needle up at 1. Wrap yarn around the needle the desired number of times and insert needle at 2, holding end of yarn with non-stitching fingers *(Fig. 9)*. Tighten knot; then pull needle through, holding yarn until it must be released.

Fig. 9

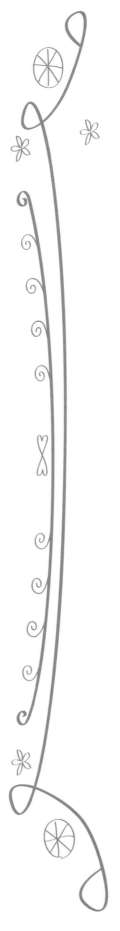

Meet Jessica Boyer

Jessica Boyer learned to crochet in childhood, taught by her grandmother, but she started crocheting more after she was diagnosed with fibromyalgia in her early twenties. "I like to make amigurumi animals that look semi-realistic and playful," she says. "This is definitely a passion for me, from sketching to crocheting to assembling the pieces."

High school sculptural work and college classes in graphic design have come in handy, she says. A stay-at-home mom, Jessica also enjoys cross stitch, wire jewelry making, and acrylic painting. More of her designs may be found in *Spirit Animals* (Leisure Arts Book #6458), *Home Team Gear* (#6695), and *Farm Animals* (#75429). She also is on Ravelry, Etsy, and jessboyercrochet.tumblr.com.

Yarn Information

The items in this book were made using medium weight yarn. Any brand of medium weight yarn may be used. A bulky weight yarn was also used for the beard/hair on the Gnome. It is best to refer to the yardage/meters when determining how many skeins or balls to purchase. Remember, to arrive at the finished size, it is the GAUGE/TENSION that is important, not the brand of yarn.

For your convenience, listed below are the yarns used to create our photography models. Because yarn manufacturers make frequent changes in their product lines, you may sometimes find it necessary to use a substitute yarn or to search for the discontinued product at alternate suppliers (locally or online).

FAWN
Red Heart® Super Saver®
Brown - #0360 Café Latte
Tan - #0334 Buff
Off White - #0316 Soft White
Black - #0312 Black

FOX
Red Heart® Super Saver®
Orange - #0256 Carrot
Black - #0312 Black
Off White - #0316 Soft White

RABBIT
Red Heart® Super Saver®
Light Brown - #0336 Warm Brown
Off White - #0316 Soft White
Pink - #0373 Petal Pink
Dark Brown - #0365 Coffee

BABY OWL
Lion Brand® Vanna's Choice®
Dark Brown - #403 Barley
Brown - #124 Toffee
Red Heart® Super Saver®
Grey - #0400 Grey Heather

GREAT HORNED OWL
Red Heart® Super Saver®
Multi - #0988 Platoon
Off White - #0316 Soft White
Black - #0312 Black
Red Heart® Classic™
Tan - #0334 Tan

FAIRY
Bernat® Super Value™
Peach - #09418 Peach
Red Heart® Super Saver®
Green - #0389 Hunter Green
White - #0311 White
Sage - #0631 Light Sage
Dark Brown - #0365 Coffee
Brown - #0360 Café Latte
Pink - #0373 Petal Pink
Dark Pink - #0706 Perfect Pink
Gold - #0321 Gold
Black - #0312 Black

GNOME
Bernat® Super Value™
Peach - #09418 Peach
Red Heart® Super Saver®
Gold - #0321 Gold
Red - #0319 Cherry Red
Dark Brown - #0365 Coffee
Brown - #0360 Café Latte
Light Brown - #0336 Warm Brown
Dark Pink - #0706 Perfect Pink
Black - #0312 Black
Red Heart® Buttercup®
White bulky - #4270 White

GNOMETTE
Bernat® Super Value™
Peach - #09418 Peach
Red Heart® Super Saver®
Yellow - #0235 Lemon
White - #0311 White
Red - #0319 Cherry Red
Brown - #0360 Café Latte
Dark Brown - #0365 Coffee
Gold - #0321 Gold
Green - #0389 Hunter Green
Dark Pink - #0706 Perfect Pink
Black - #0312 Black

Production Team: Instructional/Technical Writer - Cathy Hardy; Editorial Writer - Susan Frantz Wiles; Senior Graphic Artist - Lora Puls; Graphic Artist - Cailen Cochran; Photo Stylist - Lori Wenger; and Photographer - Jason Masters.